Billiards and Snooker

JACK KARNEHM

Pelham Books

First published in Great Britain by PELHAM BOOKS LTD
52 Bedford Square, London, W.C.1
1973

ISBN 0 7207 0360 3

*Set and printed in Great Britain by
Tonbridge Printers Ltd, Peach Hall Works, Tonbridge, Kent
in Baskerville eleven on thirteen point on paper supplied by
P. F. Bingham Ltd, and bound by Dorstel Press,
Harlow*

Contents

Twenty-four photographs and thirty
line drawings in text.

Key to balls on
line drawings:

◯ cue ball

☉ spot ball

⬤ red ball

⊗ black ball

Foreword from The Earl of Mexborough

Having had the privilege of playing with Jack Karnehm on more than one occasion, I can think of no one more fitting to write a manual on the playing of billiards and snooker than he. His break of 1,128 is an amateur billiards record, and his break of 131 at snooker is not far off one.

The late Mr Sydney Fry, who won the English Amateur Billiards Championship on seven occasions and who was a finalist in the amateur golf championship, as well as playing first-class cricket, when asked which he considered to be the most difficult game, replied without hesitation, 'Billiards'. I think this gives us some idea of the magnitude of Jack Karnehm's achievements. But not content with his playing record – and he has played in every continent – he has also taken an active part in the administration side of the game of billiards and snooker. He became Chairman of the Billiards Association and Control Council in 1968 and brought about the establishment of the present B.A.C.C. Match Hall and Office premises, and he was also instrumental in founding the present National Coaching Scheme.

Mexborough,
Arden Hall,
Helmsley, Yorks.

9

CHAPTER ONE

Technique First and Foremost

Many games are played on a billiard table, from the games of billiards and snooker to a variety of pool games. The basic skills of all are related, and the man who can wield his cue with skill should be able to play any with equal confidence and ability. His skill should show itself whatever the game.

I mention this at the outset because it is the underlying theme of this book. In writing it I have set out to teach a player how to go about acquiring good basic technique at the outset. This is the theme which I have emphasised in all my coaching, and throughout this book.

You do not become a good billiards or snooker player through learning a great variety of shots. There are millions of shots – every shot played on a table is different. How well you cope with each shot you play in a game really depends on how good your groundwork has been. Before you start to play well consistently, you must first develop a good firm stance and bridge hand, learn proper cueing control and follow through, master correct aiming, and be able to control the path of your cue ball predictably, whether it be a full ball aim straight shot or one with the control of side, screw or stun added.

Set down plainly it really seems so evident that, to play the game fluently and well, you have to have a good command of the basics. After all, to play a musical instrument well, you have to master the scales first. But from my observation of players in clubs throughout the country it is plain that this is overlooked.

For so many, the game's the thing. They do not see the necessity for any preludes.

The types of shots I describe in the following pages are predominantly intended to allow the reader to learn how to use a cue correctly, to give him a sense of control over the balls, and indeed over himself. When he has such mastery, he will be able to find the sureness of touch and power of concentration that the game demands. As confidence grows with his ability the greater his repertoire will become, and he will begin to develop his own game and style.

Looking back to the early 'thirties, which was the golden era of the game, I would say confidently that, excepting the top flight players, the overall standard of play has not really improved as much as one would have expected. In a club league match, a 40 break in snooker is a cause for celebration rather than a fairly common achievement, made by a chap with good ball sense and a natural aptitude for the game, rather than really sound technical control.

If, however, you ask a player to explain why he does certain things when he plays, he is usually quite unable to give a sound explanation. He cannot rationalise because he does not know enough about his own game. Most likely he will tell you that he plays in a particular way because he tries to play like his pal Fred, and Fred is the best player he knows. Fred, of course, is the 40-break man, but he probably has so many bad faults to offset his natural aptitude that his celebrations are few and far between!

In such ways, the pitfalls are laid. After a quick briefing on the principles of the game, a fellow starts to play, and watches others playing. Within a few weeks, having formed his own and adopted others' faults, he has begun to form a pattern which will undoubtedly set limitations for him. So the chief intention of this book is to make the reader aware of the vital importance of good technique, and that by spending some of his spare time working on it he will benefit far more than by playing billiards or snooker regardless, hoping that in the process he will suddenly get the hang of the thing and start to develop into a good player.

CHAPTER TWO

Correct Stance

It is very difficult to lay down hard and fast rules for stance, because build and length of limbs vary considerably. But there are, however, certain basic principles which are valid in all cases.

The feet should be a comfortable distance apart. The left foot should face in the general direction of the shot being played and the right foot points approximately 70 degrees to the right of that direction. Plate 1 is a good illustration of these cardinal points of a good firm stance.

Note that the weight of the body is on the back foot, the right one in this case – a most important point. In fact, I am resting on my back leg, with my left foot acting as a wedge to keep me stock still on delivery of the stroke.

This particular stance is probably more suited to billiards than snooker. There is a relaxed look about the style; it is an attitude which would aid a billiard player in the process of making a sizeable break.

I cannot over-emphasise the importance of learning to put your feet automatically in the correct position every time you visit the table. You must move the feet, not the cue, to get the right line of shot.

Be slow and meticulous while you are learning. Look at yourself. Check and recheck until it becomes part of your normal routine to adopt this position. Remember that without poise and balance your success will be very limited—however hard you try.

A slightly different stance is favoured by the general run of players, particularly snooker enthusiasts. This stance is shown in plate two.

At first glance there may appear to be little difference from the previous stance but, looking closer, you will see that the weight is transferred to the front leg, the left one, with the right leg acting as the wedge to stop any body sway on delivery of the cue.

The feet should be placed a little further apart to ensure that the weight is on the left knee, and this can be tiring at first until one becomes accustomed to it. In any case, in the initial period of getting one's stance correct, some discomfort may be experienced, such as aching muscles and tired feet, but perseverance will bring its own rewards.

The angle of the feet should again be noted : left foot pointing in the direction of the shot, right foot at approximately 70 degrees to it. Poise and balance appear to show a little more aggression, because weight is on the forward foot.

Under no circumstances, should you allow the right leg to bend at the knee (assuming, of course, that you are right-handed; the reverse naturally is the case for the left-handed player).

The very tall player with long legs who finds he has trouble getting down to the table, particularly when addressing a ball near to the cushion, will discover that by spreading his legs very wide and thrusting the bridge arm well forward from the shoulder, he can establish a solid tripod effect style which should suit him. It is important, however, that the feet are spread to take balance, to prevent side sway of the whole body when going through on the shot. This, of course, applies to all players; the aim is to be solid in style, without being cramped, though many tall men do have rather a problem in this respect.

Use of the Rest

You will undoubtedly need to use the rest many times, and you might dread the thought, particularly if you should be at a vital stage in a game, or in the middle of a nice break at billiards. So it is as well to learn the correct way to use it right from the start.

In the first place, remember that you are using the rest because you cannot reach the shot in the normal way, so there is little point in using it if you are still over-reaching. Make sure you have the right one, whether it be the half butt, the long butt, or the normal rest. But for the moment, let us consider the use of the normal rest.

The first thing to remember is that, nine times out of ten, the butt of the cue is going to be raised far more than would be the case if no rest were used. Since your cue is not going to be parallel to the table extra care has to be taken when you strike the ball to avoid any swerving of the ball. You must follow through nicely, pushing your arm right through the stroke.

A good comfortable position when playing with the rest is shown in plate 3. Note that I am playing well within myself and my cue arm can follow through to the fullest extent without my over-reaching. In the accompanying illustration, I have placed another ball beside the ball being cued to give an indication of the desired amount to follow through. Note that after the shot has been played the player should still be in a nice relaxed position, with the cue arm still not fully extended, although the follow through has been completed. The rest head should be a convenient distance from the cue ball – about 8-10 inches is average. If possible the butt of the rest itself should be lying on the table.

When using the rest, your cue arm should be turned to a different position, so that in fact it is moving parallel to the table when making the stroke. You are really using the movement from the elbow to the cue grip, just in the same way as when playing a normal stroke without the rest, but in a completely different plane (see plate 4).

CHAPTER THREE

Forming the Bridge Hand

Formation of a firm, suitable bridge hand is another important part of the framework we are building to support the cue on its line of aim.

Great care has to be taken to ensure that you are using a bridge best suited to the particular stroke you are playing. If you watch a top-class player in action, you will be impressed immediately with the strength of his bridge hand, the various ways he manipulates his fingers and thumb to help his shot. One of the surest ways to assess the calibre of a player is to watch the precision with which he puts his hand on the table.

Forming the Basic Bridge

A good sound bridge, one of the basic ones, is shown in plate 5. Fingers are well spread and the thumb is well cocked to give a good channel, or groove, for the cue to slide through. Note, also, that the thumb is pressed close to the first finger. Leaving the thumb open would allow the cue to move on the softer, or loose, skin between the fingers, causing an uneven or sticky action.

If you find it difficult to make this bridge, just smack your hand flat on the table, pressing the heel of the hand hard down. Then draw the fingers up, keeping them straight at the same time, and pressing the tips of the fingers firmly into the cloth. With a little practice you should be able to form this type of bridge properly, showing a set of clear knuckles, this indicating the pressure and firmness being applied.

I must stress again the importance of firmness for the bridge. Remember, you ought to be getting the utmost precision from yourself with every stroke played. Your eye may be able to appreciate the task in hand, but without correct technique throughout, the body will be unable to react precisely and reliably, every time.

High and Low Cue-ball Striking

It is evident that whenever the cue ball is being addressed with the bridge hand formed in this manner that to strike higher merely means you have to alter the finger position slightly. To strike lower you turn the hand over slightly, towards the ball of the thumb. For instance, should you want to strike the cue ball near the top, just draw the fingers in a little to raise the tip of the cue, perhaps about $\frac{1}{4}$ inch. To strike low, turn on to the ball of the thumb (see plate 6).

In this case more pressure has to be put on the little finger to give extra support and ensure firmness of bridge when the hand is turned over.

This type of bridge hand, with its variations for high and low cue-ball strikes, will be constantly in use when playing the general run of shots, but it will soon be found that so many curious situations can arise where good improvisation is required that I think it well worth while examining in detail some of the lesser-used bridges, as it is frequently lack of ability to improvise that brings a good break to a premature end.

The Looped Bridge

A looped bridge against the cushion is extremely useful and very often required. It is shown in plate 7. Look carefully and you will see the cue is pressed against, and slides on, the tip of the middle finger on the cushion, as near as possible to the nail where it is firm and the cue can slide freely.

Again, firmness is the keyword. Do not be frightened of pressing the cue with the looped finger to hold it firm. The thumb is tucked well out of the way on the side of the cushionrail. It would be pointless to use the looped style finger hold too loosely, allowing the cue to wander. You will automatically be able to gauge the firmness for free running of the cue.

Playing Tight on the Cushion

Probably the worst position to find yourself in, with the exception of playing over a ball, is when the cue ball is tight up on the cushion, presenting very little of its area to strike. Plate 8 shows the bridge to make. The hand is flat on the cushion rail, with the wrist dropped below the level of the cushion. Note that I am deliberately addressing the ball here with my cue running parallel to the bed of the table, thus demonstrating that it is still possible to play in the approved way from such a position. In this case little back-swing and only enough power to score would usually be called for. The cue should run on the edge of the cushion for smooth action, the bridge merely guiding the cue on line.

The Looped Finger Bridge for Potting

Of all the shots in either billiards or snooker, the pot is the most demanding of consistent accuracy. A strong bridge hand employing the looped-finger style – very widely used in the American and Continental games – keeps the cue well under control and right on the line of the stroke (see plate 9).

Compare even a simple pot with playing a losing hazard – an in-off at billiards – and you will understand the importance of learning properly how to use such a bridge which gives critical control. A losing hazard permits the use of side on the cue ball to assist it into the pocket. I will explain the effects and application of side later. Sufficient to say here that side, when imparted to the cue ball, might well allow it to spin off the jaw into the pocket. Thus, it allows a greater margin for error.

When potting a ball however, it is quite impractical to impart side to the object ball from the cue ball. Therefore, accurate central striking of the cue ball is necessary along the correct line of the stroke to ensure a successful delivery, particularly when playing an angled pot of any range. It is on such occasions that the looped-finger bridge, which keeps the cue on the line of the stroke and does not allow it to escape from the hand, can be used effectively.

Probably the time when this type of bridge is most effective is when delicate screws or very deep, powerful screw shots are being played. With such shots, the cue might escape from the hand when going through on the stroke. But, with a good strong looped-finger bridge hand, the cue is kept under control and not allowed to escape from the line of the stroke at any time during delivery.

Playing Over the Balls

Having to play over a ball, or set of balls, is a position dreaded by most players. The cue butt has to be raised which makes accurate striking extremely difficult. Once you raise the butt of the cue all sorts of complications can creep in, but, for the moment, let us just consider how the bridge should be formed, as shown in plate 10.

Observe the firmness of the fingers and the well-cocked thumb which ensures a smooth groove for the cue to slide along.

In this case, the arm has no contact with the bed of the table to aid support, so you must make the most of the position you are in, probably by leaning on the cushion rail for support, not forgetting, of course, to set your feet in the most comfortable and well-balanced position.

The angle of cueing required for this stroke is quite steep and emphasises the reason for extreme care. Place the bridge hand as close for comfort as possible to the impeding balls. By so doing you avoid having too much cue overhang from bridge to cue ball. This will help to eliminate wavering cue movement.

The more compact your entire stance is for this position, the less likelihood there is of any body movement on delivery. There is only a small area of cue ball for the cue to strike in this stroke – another very good reason why extra care and precision is needed.

A Straight Bridge Arm

For the majority of shots the bridge arm should be thrust out to its fullest extent from the shoulder and kept rigid, thereby balancing the weight of the body. It is difficult to make a hard-and-fast rule on the right position to adopt as the height of individual players varies a great deal. The player of short or medium height will probably find extra steadiness and support comes from resting part of his forearm on the table, which can be very helpful. But the tall chap often finds all of his forearm leaves the table when playing in his normal position, which can be a slight disadvantage as far as steadiness is concerned.

CHAPTER FOUR

Cue Control

The Cue Grip

The cue grip, the next important step in the formation of a sound technique, has to be firm but not too firm, the cue held lightly by all the fingers with the thumb hanging loose. Ensure that the wrist is kept in a straight line from the grip of the cue to the elbow; it must be kept in direct line with the forearm.

Any wrist movement, other than backwards or forwards on the line of the stroke, is completely incorrect, and this includes even the slightest waggling of the wrist in a circular movement.

To demonstrate the point, just let your arm hang down from the elbow quite loosely, holding an imaginary cue parallel to the table and try moving your wrist back and forth in a straight line. You will see how difficult this is; your wrist tends to develop a slight circular motion. This can cause some trouble. A wristy player can often make shots with a fluency which is undeniably good to watch, but so often his accuracy goes adrift and his inconsistency of play in general is a mystery to him.

Remember, when you set your sights on the part of the cue ball you mean to strike, only a true back and forth delivery will guarantee that you will strike that part. Such certainty, being able to guarantee your actions will have a predictable result, is what technique is all about.

I have no doubt that readers will probably find small differences in many details when starting to practise, but this is to be expected. It would be a sad thing if we all looked the same and played the same. The important thing is to understand and apply the basic techniques to the best of your ability.

Plate 11 shows a normal grip. The photo was taken with the cue in a vertical position, with the tip pointing to the ceiling. If you turn it round to the playing position with the cue parallel to the bed of the table, you will have a good view of what the correct grip should be like.

Stance and Grip – The Vital Triangle

Further reference to the grip in particular situations will be made as we progress, but here I think it would be as well if I recapped on the essential points of a good stance, as illustrated in plate 12.

The feet are comfortably spread apart; the left foot is in the general direction of the shot being played, the weight of the body on the left leg with the knee bent. The right leg is straight, acting as the wedge for rigid construction.

The left arm is fully extended from the shoulder, supported by a strong bridge hand. The forearm, from elbow to cue grip, makes a straight line, with the cue held lightly by the fingers. Note that the cue is running parallel to the bed of the table forming a triangle from the cue grip, which we shall call point A, to the bridge hand, point B, with a line running from B through the shoulders to point C at the elbow of the cueing arm.

This triangle is the picture you should try to keep in your mind as a reference for all your future playing. It is with this framework of A,B,C, in conjunction with the placing of your feet, legs and body, that will aid improvement.

Note also in plate 12 how my chin is well down on the cue, and my forearm gives added support on the table. It can now be appreciated that with a framework well constructed and securely fixed, the cue can be propelled surely on the line of aim by swinging in a forward motion from point *C*, the elbow. This forward swing has to be smooth and without any unnecessary movement of the body such as raising the head, or the slightest movement of the legs and feet. In fact one must try to be like a statue.

When practising the cue swing, it is most important to try to limit the backward swing of the cue as much as possible. The less backswing the better, particularly when power is used.

Back Swing

During my visits to various halls and clubs I have often become involved in discussions about the game in general and how different types of players play in particular. The variety of opinions concerning cue action especially surprises me. It does seem that this is a very neglected area of information in the game, and I can only conclude that a little knowledge has proved to be dangerous.

Snooker players, in their determination to make their mark in the club, maybe with higher aspirations to league or county level, have thought a lot about why they miss some apparently easy shots and have probably come to the conclusion that if they can cut down on the back swing of their action they will eliminate the error of bad cue-ball striking on the point of delivery. They may be right to some extent, but in considering this alone they are only tackling one small facet of a very complex question.

In a player's efforts to refrain from any back swing – starting the forward movement of the cue with the cue arm hanging in the vertical position from the elbow – it is the easiest thing in the world to develop the short little jab stroke. For potting only, especially the shorter distances, this jab stroke may give a certain degree of efficiency, but when you study the cue-ball position and control which should also be part of the shots, it is evident that much more is necessary. By developing this short jab method the action is likely to become stunted, and the push through of the cue in the follow through, after the cue ball has been struck, will be neglected. In other

23

words, the action has been cut short at the beginning and end of the delivery. This is a natural, though not a good, thing to do.

You will generally find it is only the top-flight players who execute this smooth action with regularity and consistency, and this is because of the many hundreds of hours of planned and methodical practice behind them, practice which is a very tiring task. But persistence pays off, resulting in good habits which allow you to play each shot naturally and without conscious effort. A cue action should be a smooth, well-timed, unhurried delivery, keeping the cue on the bridge hand, on the line of aim, with the cue as parallel to the table as possible (if the shot demands this). If you make it a rule never to move from the stroke until you have seen the result of the shot you have played, you will find many of these problems easier to tackle.

The top player is constantly watching for any lapse of self discipline in his stance at the table and in his approach and control. The player who naturally just drops into a good style and appears to play all the shots with little or no back swing and a good follow through is a rarity indeed, believe me. So my advice to all players is to develop an awareness of technique and style, but do not be obsessed with it. When you are playing the game, play it freely and do not worry too much about the back swing, to a point where you are thinking more about your elbow than the shot in hand. Get on with the game, and try to win, but gradually apply little modifications which will get you nearer to the ultimate. True perfection is virtually unobtainable, of course, but as your standard improves, so room for further improvement becomes less.

So remember, a fine cue action must also be coupled to a good, solid, well-balanced style. One is no good without the other. I repeat, that if you practise properly, and by that I mean with determination and purpose, concentrating on what you are doing, it is bound to come through in your play later on. So when you play, play seriously, but enjoy it and let your practice come through naturally. Plate 13 will convey to you many of the points mentioned.

The Six-Shot – A Stern Test

Playing a six-shot will give you the chance to practise your action. The idea of the shot is to test to the full every facet of your cue action and technique. I must stress that, in practising this shot, you are unlikely to be successful very often. But the main idea is to reveal the errors you are making, to note if they are consistent errors, and then to work on eliminating them.

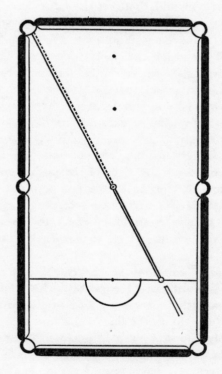

FIG 1.

Place the red ball on the middle spot and the cue ball on the baulk line in a direct line with the top and bottom pockets (Figure 1). The purpose of this shot is to pot the red ball into

25

the top pocket, seeing if you can follow through and cause the white to enter the pocket as well – in other words, a six-shot.

Doubtless, if I removed the red from the spot and asked you to strike the cue ball into the top pocket without touching the jaws you will do it every time. So, if I replace the red in the path of the cue ball, why should you not be able to pot the red every time and, for that matter, the cue ball as well, getting the six-shot? The answer, of course, is that this demands extremely accurate striking and a very good delivery.

Correct Striking

As likely as not you will find that, on the occasions that you pot the red, the cue ball will go to one side of the pocket or the other with fair consistency. You may also find that the cue ball tends hardly to reach the pocket. You may find that, on most of the occasions that you miss the pot, the object ball goes to one particular side of the pocket.

All these things will tell you just what you are doing wrong in your delivery and give you a clue on just how to correct any faults. The shot has to be played with central striking. Should you strike slightly to the left of your cue ball this will throw the red slightly to the right of the pocket, and striking right of the cue ball will throw the red or object ball to the left of the pocket. If you strike below centre you will find that this will tend to give a stunning effect to the cue ball and you will lose run on it, which means that it may not reach the pocket.

On the other hand, you may strike centrally on the cue ball and find that you still miss the pocket. This could mean that you did not have the cue on the line of the stroke – the butt must be behind the tip on the line of the stroke.

However, suddenly you will get a beauty which makes both balls disappear smartly into the top pocket. It is a reward which makes you feel you have proved something, and you will find that practice makes such rewards more frequent. From personal experience I have found that when I am striking this shot well in practice and getting it fairly frequently,

I feel it is because my timing is good; I am getting that follow through running sweetly and my body is as solid as a rock.

If, however, you feel that this shot is too difficult for your particular stage of development, give yourself a better chance by placing the red ball on the centre spot and putting the cue ball 18 inches behind it, across the table between the centre pockets (Figure 2), and carry out the same operation, trying to get the six-shot into the middle pocket. The same principles apply, except that you are closer to the balls, which, of course, is helpful and means that the chance of error is lessened to a certain extent, and being closer to the shot you will see what is happening a little more clearly.

There is no doubt that of all the shots, the winning hazard demands the highest possible accuracy of cue-ball striking and

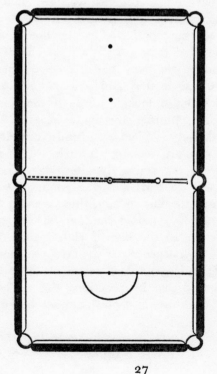

FIG 2.

delivery. I have discovered over the years when coaching, a very common fault concerning getting on the line creeps into a pupil's game. If he is not made aware of it, it can become a built-in hazard. To overcome this particular difficulty, which is most evident when playing length-of-the-table shots, I have evolved a little routine over the years which I have found very helpful indeed.

For instance, if we take a long pot with the red on the middle spot and the cue ball on the baulk line, the normal routine would be to survey the shot standing back and then to step into the shot, getting down into position for cueing. I suggest that once you are into cueing position you just look at the cue ball and nowhere else, without looking along the line of the shot. Commence cueing with the backwards and forwards motion, with the cue addressing the cue ball to strike it in the centre.

Now, when you have made sure that you are cueing in the centre, just look up without any further movement and see how near you are to being perfectly on the line of the shot. Most players, if they find they are slightly off the line of the shot, will tend to make the very slightest correction without moving their feet. Consider this, and you will realise that if you do this whilst you are looking through the line of the shot, you are, in fact, putting the body in an off-balance position for your delivery. When you find yourself in this position, it means you are looking through the line of the shot, but pointing your cue across that imaginary line, to the right or left. The way to correct this is to move your feet, bringing the cue on to the line of aim, thus ensuring that you are in a balanced and well-poised position for delivery, with the butt behind the tip on the line of aim. I think you will find this will help to sharpen your reflexes on the drill of aiming on the shot, and also to be aware of the position of your feet. You will find that by practising this method, your table approach will improve and your aiming become surer.

CHAPTER FIVE

Mastering the Principles of Aiming

Basic Stroke Practice

How well you have mastered a good stance and position, formation of a firm, basic bridge hand, and correct cue action
can best be observed, and errors corrected, by practising striking a ball straight up and down the table, over the spots. First,
make the stroke with a smooth and gentle delivery, endeavour-
ing to make the cue ball return to the cue tip. Then gradually
increase power until the ball travels four times up and down
the table. There is little point in actually playing scoring strokes,
since this requires concentration on other matters than straight-
forward striking of the cue ball.

Bear in mind only that you are trying to establish a firm
base from which to work, and single-minded perseverance –
and this basic stroke practice will take time – will be well
rewarded later.

When you feel that you are beginning to master the stroke,
and you feel also that your understanding of your stance is
improving, move the ball to another part of the baulk line and
repeat the drill, hitting the ball up the table, and remaining
in the striking position, seeing if you can bring the ball back to
your cue tip.

It is more difficult without the spots to help your aim. You
will find, however, that with practice you will soon begin to
align yourself correctly for the shot. When you can do this
consistently you are on the way to better things.

Forcing Strokes

You will find that driving the cue ball up over the spots to complete four lengths of the table needs far more power than just the plain two length stroke. It calls for a forcing stroke. It is most important in a forcing stroke to make sure that you have plenty of follow through – you must let your cue go right through on delivery of the stroke.

Now, in this case, when the forearm is moved forward with the delivery and gets to the end of its run, you should break the shoulder-to-elbow line and allow the arm to continue further through the stroke. This will give you more power and more follow through.

Plate 14 shows this to advantage. Notice particularly how the head is kept down with the chin on the cue, the cue remaining parallel to the table, and the flexing of the wrist to allow the cue to go through to its utmost limit. The bridge hand must not move at all.

Forcing strokes are the shots which will highlight any weaknesses in your stance and your technique, because, on playing a shot with power, the body is more likely to be thrown off balance a little with the physical effort involved. So before playing any shot that demands some degree of power make sure that your feet are firmly planted on the ground, that your bridge hand is very firm and, in fact, get as solid and as comfortable as you can so that the physical effort made in delivering the cue does not in any way take it off the line of aim.

Timing

Before we go on to our first exercise shot, it would be as well to explain the principles of aiming and the mental approach involved which, put in simple terms, really means timing. Timing is an expression used by so many sportsmen, when discussing the techniques of golf, cricket, football, tennis, and many other sports. Timing can either make or break your efforts.

It is when your game is flowing that your timing is good.

Everything comes easily, you do everything perfectly; in fact, you are in form. You feel great, you do not even have to think about it, it just happens. However, it is still vital to understand what is happening when you are in such confident mood, and why.

The Aiming Sequence

I can best analyse the essentials of correct, confident aiming by describing the sequence of events involved in a simple shot like potting the black from its spot, the cue ball being two feet behind it, on a line with the corner pocket. In the approved style you get down to the stroke, checking to make sure that you are striking the cue ball in the centre by aiming your tip at it, lining up with a backward and forward motion, maybe three or four times.

Having satisfied yourself that all is right, your eyes go forward to the black, or object ball, to see that your line of aim, right through the stroke to the pocket, is correct. Then your eyes re-check that you are still striking the cue ball in the centre. If all these conditions are right you have taken aim correctly and are ready to deliver.

Now, for a fraction of a second, you pause. Having committed yourself to your shot, you look at the object ball, keep your eyes glued on the ball, and without hesitation and full of confidence let your cue slide through to pot the black.

You will see that I have split the shot into two separate operations. First is the taking aim, which automatically includes stance and alignment of the cue on the line of the shot, and double checking. Then comes the pause, followed by playing the shot. It is at this pause point that you have brought all your reflexes to a peak when they must be released – and that is the moment of truth.

This, of course, seems a lot to say, but, in fact, happens in every stroke which is played. The reason that there are fast and slow players, is that the preparation of aim varies in individuals and so does the pulling of the trigger. Whether approach is fast or slow, there has to be flow between the two phases. It is when there is not that you miss, the result being worse in some cases than others. Maybe you hesitate too long before firing or perhaps division of concentration between cue ball and object ball is not perfectly co-ordinated. If you are looking towards the pocket, glancing again at the cue ball, or doubting your ability to play the stroke perfectly, you are compromising your chance of success at the stroke.

Concentration, keeping your mind solely on one task, refusal to be distracted, and determination, are all vital. A good temperament, so that you are not easily put off, is a real asset.

Cue Follow Through

Plates 15, 16 and 17 show the cue delivery and follow through when a shot is being played; this is the general type of shot, showing all points to advantage, particularly addressing the cue ball with the cue when it is parallel to the table. I must keep stressing this point as it is very important.

The bridge hand should be a nice comfortable distance from the cue ball, giving just the right overhang of the cue. The follow through after delivery is shown and it should be noted that the cue is still on the bridge hand. This is also extremely important. Also the cue is parallel to the table, a very difficult part of cueing when you are going through a shot; a habit which should be cultivated in one's own style and technique. By doing this, you are applying self-discipline by not moving on the stroke and being aware of yourself – your own presence at the table. This is a facet of the game vital to the successful player in every phase of the game.

Note, also, the head is still down on the cue. You will see many players – good, bad and indifferent – and you will notice how, when they have finished their stroke, the positioning of the body has changed completely, their cue is pointing to the sky – in fact, it may be pointing anywhere, and you may find that they appear to get reasonable results. They might be quite good players, but do not let this deter you in any way as, after

32

Plate 1. A relaxed but firm position, weight on straight back leg, left foot facing shot. Right foot angled, to counter body sway. Soften all finger cue grip, chin well down on cue. Cue parallel to bed of table.

Plate 2. Weight on front leg, back leg straight, feet further apart.

Plate 3. Comfort, no over-reaching, rest butt on table. Cue arm parallel to table bed.

Plate 4. No over-reaching or body movement. Rest head in low position for normal shot.

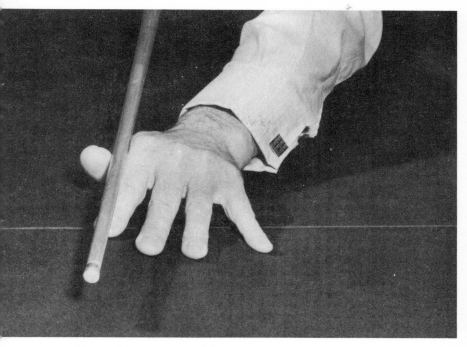

Plate 5. Firm well spread fingers, thumb close to forefinger.

Plate 6. As 5, except the hand is turned on the ball of the thumb, pressure on little finger, thumb dropped.

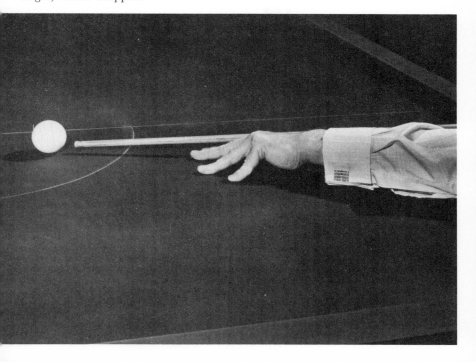

Plate 7. Looped finger holding cue against middle finger; i.e. cue parallel to table.

Plate 8. Dropped wrist, weight forward on bridge hand.

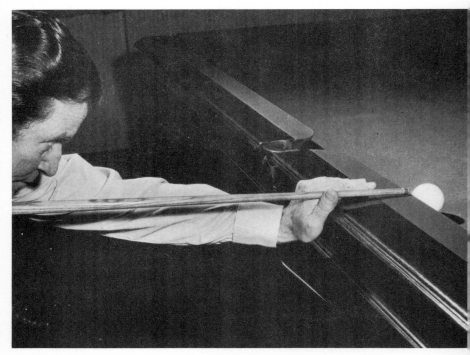

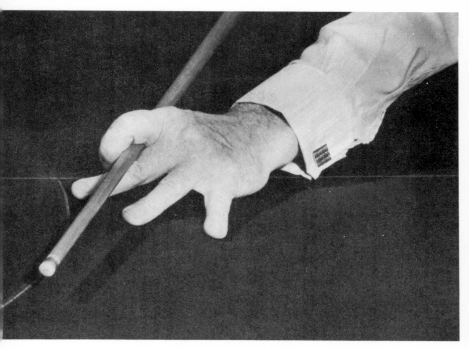

Plate 9. Fingers well spread, cue held firmly in loop.

Plate 10. Bridge close as possible to cue ball and very firm, indicated by knuckles. Well cocked thumb.

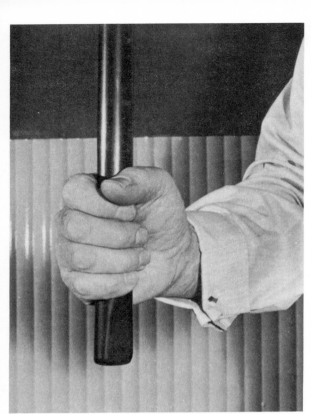

Plate 11. All fingers grip. Light. Loose thumb.

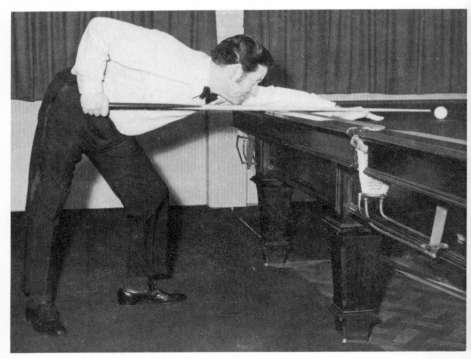

Plate 12. Feet position good, legs correct for forward balance. Cue parallel to table, forming A.B.C. triangle. All fingers cue grip, firm bridge hand. Chin well down.

Plate 13. Bridge hand firm, cue grip light but firm. Bridge arm thrust well forward. A.B.C. Stroke completed.

Plate 14. Follow through complete after forcing stroke, wrist flexed forward. Note chin and cue positions, and shoulder to elbow angle.

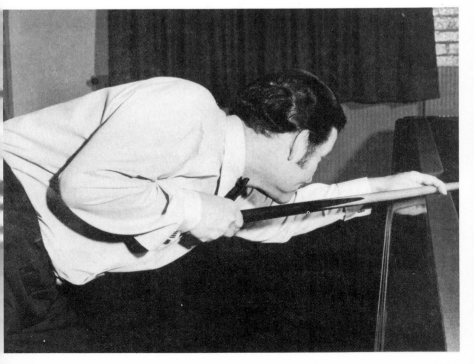

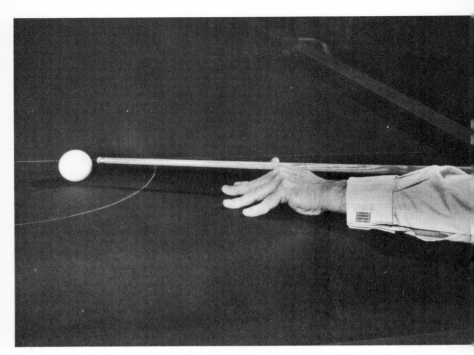

Plate 15. Addressing cue ball.

Plate 16. Ready to strike.

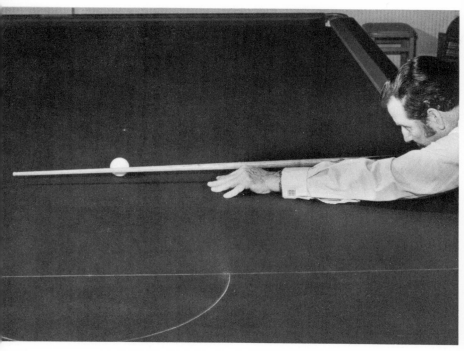

Plate 17. Stroke completed. Note follow through, and all points before and after completion. (15—16—17.)

Plate 18. Using the wrong rest; over reaching; off balance.

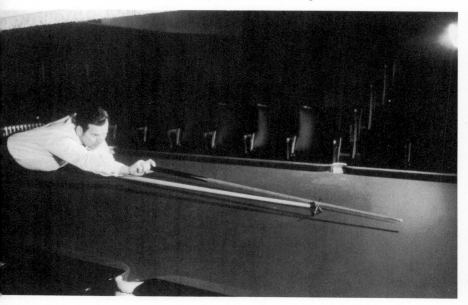

Plate 19. A.B.C. incorrect, chin, wrist, head, all out of line.

Plate 20. Same shot, back on the line.

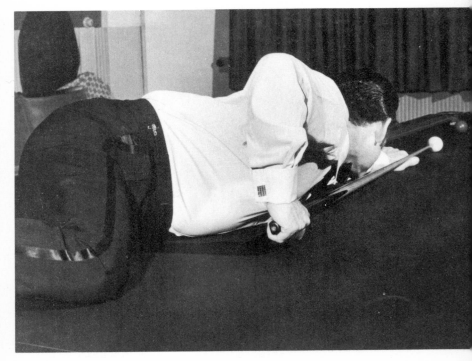

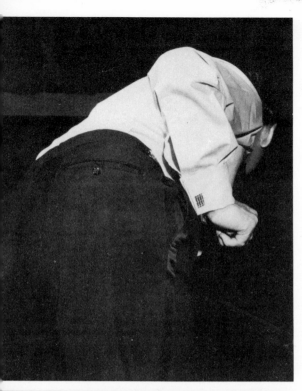

Plate 21. A common fault, worth correcting.

Plate 22. 21 corrected, note light cue grip, loose thumb.

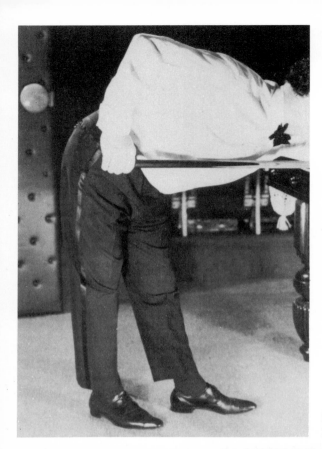

Plate 23. Feet incorrect, grip wrong and out of line, both legs straight.

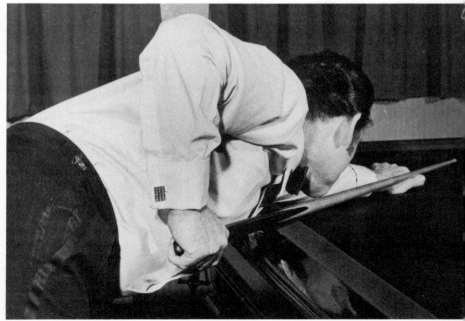

Plate 24. A.B.C. and dead on line

all, we are trying to show the correct way of doing things, and this should be the ultimate aim for anybody wishing to improve.

Style

Showing style at the table is a great help to a player. It breeds confidence and at times has just the reverse effect on your opponent. Remember that if you pay constant attention to technique and your styling, and being precise in your actions, at all times, you will feel the benefit when you are playing under a strain, when the game may be very, very tight and the pressure is on. This is where self-discipline will stand you in good stead.

Perhaps this is an appropriate moment to point out why I am putting so much stress on developing techniques at the outset, rather than just playing the game and hoping. It should now be apparent that if you can combine stance and your table approach and good aiming procedure with correct, assured delivery, then the success of the shot is almost a formality, a natural end product.

Consistency

In the next few chapters I shall describe how you should go about mastering a number of key shots, marrying correct technique to the right approach, so that you build up a solid armoury of shots. The more consistent you become at playing them, the more confident your game will be.

As you progress with your cue power and control, the array of shots you can create will allow you to progress further still. You may meet and talk with players who will say 'Oh, I'm trying to improve my technique so much that I can't think of the shots when I'm playing' and this can very well be true in many cases, but this is the very reason why I want you to get your technique correct at the start so that as you progress you begin to get involved in the game. Because of your initial efforts to perfect your stance and technique as much as possible, you will gradually forget about having to check such points when you are playing the shots and getting involved in the game.

Then you will begin to apply your concentration and your efforts automatically to the shot itself.

Of course, as you begin to get good results from your game, you may have lapses of form. That is when you should turn back and brush up on the little routine exercises which helped you to develop good technique. It is a matter of getting priorities right; eliminating inconsistencies of play is really the success secret of the professional. Even though you may have no ambitions to become a professional, you will find you get far more pleasure from the sport by adopting correct methods, and better results.

A Test of Aiming

It should be apparent by now, that the cue, though it is no magic wand, plays a big part in helping you to take aim and make your cue ball strike a desired spot on any section of another ball or point on a cushion. It is not accurate enough merely to take casual aim and then strike the ball in the direction you have decided upon. It is most important to look through, and right into, the shot. Make the eyes search out that vital, so elusive, spot. The sooner you learn to appreciate this vital aspect, the sooner will all the various facets of your delivery – getting down on the shot, preamble, delivery, sighting, and final execution – slot into place, giving you perfect aiming of the stroke. To help your understanding of this, try the following routine.

Make a chalk mark on the side cushion 15 inches above the middle pocket. With the cue ball on the corner of the 'D' nearest the cushion marked, aim at this chalk mark at normal pace and mark where the ball strikes the bottom cushion. I am prepared to bet that you hit the cushion in front of the mark. Now play again, this time taking into account the diameter of the $2\frac{1}{16}$ inch ball, aim your cue just past the mark, through the centre of the cue ball, allowing the outside of your ball to strike the mark. You will now see that the angle taken is not quite so sharp as you thought and the cumulative effect over some 20 feet or more can be considerable. This is

34

the importance of true sighting, and alignment of shot, which is the beginning and end of potting in particular. Remember when trying this test that pace will alter the angle of throw by the cushions and, of course, that central striking must be made.

CHAPTER SIX

Practice Shots for Improving Technique

To aid the development of sound technique and good style, it is necessary to have a set of fundamental shots on which to build. The first ones you should learn to cope with are basic winning and losing hazards, with central, accurate cue-ball striking being the vital necessity. All the features of a good action can be studied in this series. From these it is possible to make a practice hazard break of any magnitude, according to your ability, which, if pursued, will assist tremendously with concentration, continuity of play, in fact all the assets required in breakmaking.

The method of aiming for the losing half-ball hazard is the really important factor, which lays the foundations for all your future aiming and getting on the line of the shot. The tip of your cue must be aimed through the centre of the cue ball, at the edge of the object ball you intend to strike. Remember also that the line formed must also continue back along your cue to the butt in your hand. In other words the whole length of the cue is also straight on that continued line of aim; the butt must be behind the tip on the line of the shot.

Accuracy of Delivery

The first stroke to incorporate regularly in your practice is one which, when mastered, will allow you to play competently the half ball stroke, particularly important for losing hazard, or in-off scoring, and delivering on the line of the stroke.

On a marked spot, $16\frac{3}{4}$ inches below the centre spot of the

36

table, I want you to place the red billiard ball. Now, from either corner of the 'D', you will have half-ball aim in-off into either middle pocket; from the left-hand side of the 'D' into the right-hand middle pocket, and from the right-hand side of the 'D' into the left-hand middle pocket (Figure 3).

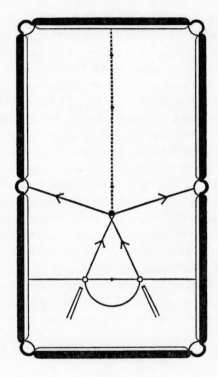

FIG 3.

Having put your cue ball on one of the corner spots of the 'D', take a half-ball aim and play an in-off the red into the middle pocket. If your aim is executed accurately, the red or object ball will travel in a straight line up the table and return on the same line from the top cushion.

The shot itself is a comparatively easy one which you should soon be able to get. The important thing, however, is to be able to play the shot at the right strength to bring the red back to the original spot for a repeat of the shot.

At first you will probably find that you can get the shot quite easily, but either the red will stop in one of many positions after contact, so you have to begin to apply some thought to positioning for subsequent shots.

Playing for instance from the right of the 'D' it is evident that, if the object ball travels to the left of the straight line, you have made a contact which is too thick, and to the right of the line, a contact which is too thin – too glancing a blow. You must strike your cue ball in the centre, and just fractionally high. Should you unintentionally strike the ball to the left of centre it will tend to throw square and, after contact with the red, will hit the first jaw of the pocket. In billiard language this means you have used running side. Make a similar error to the right and you will find it will go from the object ball to strike the far jaw. This means you have used check side.

Now the sooner you are able to apply your technique and strike accurately on the line of aim, with the butt of the cue directly behind the tip, the sooner you will be able to gauge the strength of the shot, and you will have a shot in your repertoire which you can carry off reliably. Again, I stress, remember at this early stage that all your actions tend to be habit-forming. So do not forget to follow through, do not raise your head on the stroke, and try to keep your cue on the bridge hand. Do not let your eye follow the cue ball into the pocket either – it is important to keep your vision on the line of the shot.

At this stage a little exaggeration in performing such actions will not hurt. For instance, make it a rule never to move a muscle until you have seen the result of your shot from the delivery position, when you are down on the cue. This may be very demanding, but is invaluable if carried out. This shot should be played and replayed until you feel confidence coming into your delivery, and the half-ball angle is imprinted on your mind.

Gradually, you will find that the slight adjustments in aiming that you are making to endeavour to keep the red ball straight up and down the table will assist your powers of concentration. You will be amazed how the effort will tire you, but at the same time it will give you great satisfaction as you gradually achieve a certain amount of success.

The great beauty of this shot and, indeed, the other shots we are going to play from the half-ball angle, is that the defects of your delivery of the cue, of your aiming and striking of the cue ball, are revealed to you by the path and the final positioning of the red. Ultimately, you will find that, by being able to bring the red ball back close to the marked spot, you will instinctively reposition your cue ball to the necessary position on the 'D' line, so that when you play the next shot you will again bring the red ball back; that continuity of play is beginning to come into your scheme of thinking as well.

The Middle Pocket Cross Loser

For the next practice shot I want you to place the red ball on the billiard spot and place the white ball anywhere on an imaginary line drawn from the billiard spot to the upper shoulder of the middle pocket (Figure 4). A beginner will find it will be as well to place the white ball somewhere on this line that will enable him to be able to get his hand comfortably on the table, so that he can take up quite a good, normal stance.

So placed, he is in a position to play the next half-ball stroke. Again, the outcome of the next shot will be governed by the positioning of the red ball after the stroke has been played. The red should travel to the top cushion and return down over the spots while, of course, your white ball enters the top corner pocket of the table, on whichever side you are playing. Ideally, the red should travel down the table, over the spots, and stop on the precise spot that we played shot number one from.

I want you to play this stroke quite a few times, putting the cue ball in various positions along the line of aim until you have become thoroughly acquainted with the sighting and strength of shot, and can reposition the red ball very close to the initial starting spot position. You should then play from

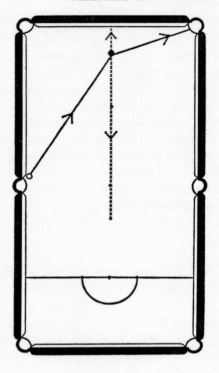

FIG 4.

the other side of the table, from varying positions, until you can produce equivalent results.

The thing to watch here is that, though it may appear strange, you will probably find you play with more ease on one side of the table than you do on the other. When playing from your 'uneasy' side, you must just knuckle down and try that little bit harder, until you begin to play the shot as well as from your best side.

The most difficult variation of this shot is playing it when the white ball is as far as it can be from the red, i.e. on the knuckle of the cushion by the centre pocket. This means that cueing is not quite so free because you cannot get your hand on the table to give yourself a good bridge.

Playing from this position highlights the importance of steadiness of the body, with the feet nicely planted on the floor, and a sound bridge hand. So do not shirk playing the shot from such positions either side of the table; it is of particular value in making you a little more aware of any weakness in your stance.

At first you should play this stroke at natural strength. With this particular shot we can also apply a forcing stroke, which will give you an indication of how you can alter the angle of throw of your cue ball by applying force. You must still aim with the same accuracy, the object ball following the same path after contact, indicating the trueness of your delivery.

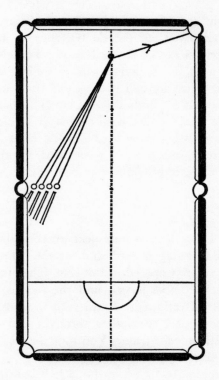

FIG 5.

To do this, gradually move the cue ball out from the knuckle of the centre pocket a couple of inches (Figure 5). You will then find that with just a little extra force on the stroke – allowing the cue to do the work, remember – you will swing the cue

41

ball into the top pocket and the red ball will travel in the same path, up and down over the spots, this time probably going into the baulk and coming out just over the baulk line from the bottom cushion.

From this you will find that by placing the cue ball even a little wider, say 3 inches maybe to 5 inches, you need more of a forcing stroke to swing the ball in, in other words to make the cue ball throw a wider angle, but remember, in doing this, you should not alter the path of the red ball, which is always the indicator to the accuracy of your stroke.

When you have played at this stroke for a while I am quite sure you will begin to appreciate just how difficult it is to make the object ball travel to the desired spot on one occasion, let alone after a series of shots. I emphasise this because I do not want you to be despondent after failing and think 'Well, I can't play, I just haven't got a clue,' because the fact is that even the top player finds this extremely difficult.

In fact, it is most unlikely that the best player would be able to do what I am suggesting consistently, unless he is feeling in the best of form and things are going his way. In striving for such perfection you are improving your own stance and techniques.

The Half-ball Long Loser

The half-ball long losing hazard, our next practice shot, is undoubtedly the hardest losing hazard shot for the simple reason that slightly more power is needed in this shot. The cue ball has to travel much farther to its target, and the red ball in turn has further to travel after impact. Extra care is needed on the free delivery of the stroke, the follow through, and in maintaining the steadiness of your frame. You must be sure to strike the ball above the centre.

Figure 6 shows the correct position for a half-ball in-off into the top pocket either side of the table. The red should be placed on the centre spot of the table, and the cue ball $2\frac{1}{4}$ inches from the corner of the 'D' on the baulk line.

The build up to the stroke needs to be gradual; try to play

the stroke gently, just allowing the white ball to reach the top pocket and fall in, without worrying at all where the red ball goes. Then gradually increase the pace – and do not be impatient about this – until you begin to feel the strength of the shot.

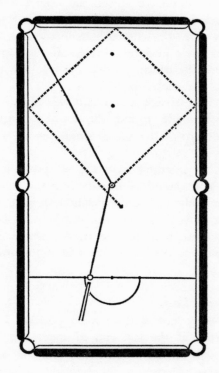

Fig 6.

Now, having played this several times for as long as your patience will allow, you will find that for correct half-ball contact the line of aim is to point your cue through the centre of the cue ball, aiming the cue at the edge of the red object ball and delivering through on the line of the shot.

You will find that the probable path of the red ball is via the side cushion, the top cushion and around to the other side cushion, with red eventually stopping near the centre side pocket, leaving it in a position – if play were being continued – where you could have either another in-off into the middle pocket or a long loser into the top pocket, if the object ball stopped somewhere in the region of the centre spot.

Once again, it can be seen that the path of the red ball is the indicator of how you have struck the object ball in the first place. Too thick a contact would mean that you would drive the red ball to strike the side cushion further up the table, thereby altering the angle and bringing it off the top cushion further down towards the centre pocket, possibly leaving a pot red from hand into the centre pocket.

If, however, you have struck it too thin, the object ball will take a more square angle round the cushions, and come to rest nearer the centre of the table, almost on to the centre spot.

The shot should be practised from the set position as long as patience allows. You should eventually find the red ball returning to approximately the same position, which indicates that your striking and your aim is becoming fairly consistent in this stroke. The more you practise it, the clearer will the image be printed on your mind, which will automatically increase your confidence.

The Top-pocket Cross Loser

The last half-ball losing hazard from a set position I propose to deal with is played at the top end of the table. For this shot, place the red ball on the billiard spot and the white ball tight against the top cushion on the knuckle of the pocket (Figure 7), in a position where you are just not angled for striking the red ball. (You *are* angled, and hence in a position which prevents direct play, if the cue ball is so far into the pocket that it would be deflected off the aim to the object ball by the pocket knuckle.)

From this position, by striking half ball on the red, you will go in-off in the opposite top pocket, sending the red ball down the table towards the centre pocket, striking the side cushion approximately 18 inches above the centre pocket, coming off the cushion towards the centre of the table for an in-off from hand into the middle pocket.

This shot is generally termed the cross losing hazard. You will observe that the shot is at a rather more acute angle than any other we have dealt with so far, therefore the margin of error is less. One has to pay a great deal of care and attention to the accurate striking of the cue ball. To make matters more tricky, the bridging for this shot can be just a little bit difficult as you are not able to get your hand on the table.

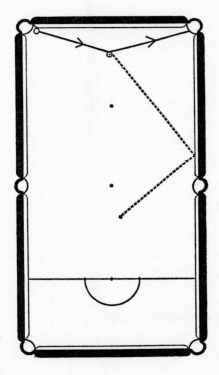

Fig 7.

Pace can be a very deceiving factor with this shot. The right pace for the stroke will ensure that the red ball travels far enough to get past the middle pocket off the side cushion to leave you the in-off from hand.

Linking the Shots

Having now completed our four losing hazard shots, let us assume that, after a considerable amount of practice, we have achieved a certain degree of efficiency, and that when playing the long loser from hand particularly we have learnt that we can still get the shot, although we may hit the object ball a little thicker or thinner, which shows there is some latitude for error.

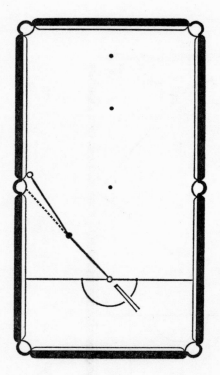

FIG 8.

The next object is to try and link these four shots together so that you create greater interest in your practice and begin to have continuity of play. This will help you to get used to playing at the table for reasonably long periods, playing from positions made entirely by your own efforts and not from set marks.

46

Playing Winning Hazards

To achieve greater continuity we have to play one or two shots which are referred to as winning hazards, as opposed to the losing hazards that we have played so far. A winning hazard is when you pot the object, not the cue ball, into the pocket.

The shot I want you to practise next is a winning hazard, potting the red into the centre pocket. The red is placed half-way on a line drawn from the centre pocket to the middle spot of the 'D', the white or cue ball, is on the centre spot of the 'D' (Figure 8). I want you to allow the cue ball to run through and just go to the knuckle – the upper jaw – of the centre pocket.

Now this is a relatively easy stroke and, if you wish, can be varied by placing the red ball in different positions along the line, potting it into the centre pocket, making the cue ball run to the same spot on the top of the centre pocket and remaining there. For the cue ball to run through nicely, having potted the red, you must follow through, striking the ball fractionally above centre and letting the cue do the work; you need a free cueing action.

If you next place the red on the billiard spot and the cue ball 2 feet behind it on a line with the top corner pocket either side of the table (Figure 9), you will have a very similar winning hazard shot to the one just described, this time placed for potting the red into the top corner pocket. It will allow the cue ball to run through again on to the top cushion close to the jaw of the pocket, which will leave you with the cross losing hazard position already described.

Bear in mind all the time that these shots I have described are, first and foremost, good vehicles for observing how well you are coping with your stance and cueing action, aiming and timing. Preoccupation with such matters does seem to be neglected among billiards and snooker players. By way of contrast, the outlook of golf enthusiasts, to quote one instance, seems refreshingly different. They will naturally be interested in the outcome of a stroke or series of strokes, in say, the different routes Jacklin, Nicklaus and Player take to the 11th at

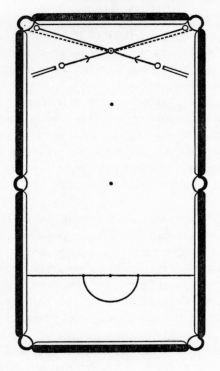

FIG 9.

St Andrews. But they seem keener on studying minutely the way each player tees off, gets out of the rough, or putts. In short, there is an interest in the means rather than the end product.

Playing a Sequence

You can now see, with the series of shots we have just learnt to play competently, that it is quite possible to build up a break of winning or losing hazards of almost any size, depending entirely upon the ability of the player. Now, just to prove this, let us run through an imaginary sequence of shots which could be played by a player of high standard, assuming his accuracy is going to be pretty good, and see what can happen.

Let us start by placing the red for the long loser position, red on centre spot, cue ball $2\frac{1}{4}$ inches from the corner of the

'D'. The shot is played and the red ball travels round the table, coming to halt, leaving a neat middle pocket loser from hand. This leaves us with the ordinary middle pocket loser, a shot which can be repeated many times, according to the ability of the player, until a bad stroke is made. We will assume, however, that the red comes too far down the table, which means that the in-off into the middle pocket is not possible.

We now find that the red can be potted into the middle pocket, and if we make the cue ball run through to the top knuckle of this centre pocket we are well placed for an in-off the red from the billiard spot. With this shot we can bring the red ball down over the centre spots to a position for another in-off into the middle pocket.

In playing the next middle pocket loser, we find that we have played under strength and that the red, although it has gone up the table nicely over the spots, has only returned close to the centre spot. Still, we are able to play the long loser from hand, making slight variations of adjustment to our cue ball in an effort to bring the red ball again round the table for a further losing hazard. Not a bad break, is it?

From this sequence you can see that while, naturally, there will be variations and you may break down many times in your efforts to get such a sequence of shots going, you will begin to understand and cope with the various angles confronting you in your efforts to keep the break going. The whole point is that you are now playing with a purpose. You have some reference points on the table where you can put your cue ball when playing a given shot, knowing that if you pull it off you can continue the break and you will be surprised how this will spur you on and give you something to go for when you are practising. It makes play far more interesting.

For the enthusiast who wants to play billiards, there is a mine of information in the few shots that we have played, and I have no doubt that anybody with imagination and a little aptitude for billiards will find so many variations and different ways of commencing a break of hazard play, that he will find his practice time passing very quickly indeed, with the intense concentration he is going to need.

However, the snooker enthusiast might feel that he is not so well catered for with this repertoire. But he is, really, if you bear in mind that I have emphasised that the purpose behind all our practice so far has been to improve stance, cue action, approach and all the other basic points of correct play. I am quite sure that the snooker player, after practice of this nature, must find that when he goes back to his snooker his improvement will be most marked. Generally speaking, I think it would be fair criticism to say that the cue action of most snooker players is short and rather jerky, and does not have the fluency that it should have.

CHAPTER SEVEN

Effects of Side, Screw and Stun

No doubt you will have noticed that every shot we have discussed playing so far has called for plain ball striking, not involving side in any way, although I have no doubt it has been applied quite unintentionally many times during your practice sessions! I hope you will have been aware of this, and tried to get the cue running through directly on the line of the stroke.

Applying Side

Now the application of side in itself is not difficult, but to be able to apply side with definite control for positional purposes is quite a different thing. The subtle effects of side are so fascinating and delightful when you are able to employ them with a fair degree of accuracy.

So much could be written on the effects, powers and possibilities of side. This is of greatest interest to the billiard player, because there is a tremendous variety of shots and strokes in billiards that demand the subtle use of side for various reasons. In snooker, however, good accurate striking is the secret of success and wherever possible it is best to avoid the use of side. As he becomes more proficient, a snooker player will try more sophisticated shots and sometimes he will want to apply side deliberately for positional purposes. So to become a good class snooker player it is essential to have a sound command of side and all its varying effects.

At first, most beginners find it difficult to apply side when aiming, but a little careful thought will help you to cope. First

you take your aim through the centre of the cue ball in the
normal way. Having established your line of aim, you move the
cue tip to the part of the ball you wish to strike to apply side,
making sure – and this is very important – that you keep the
cue parallel to the original line of aim. You will then be set
for your shot. This is a routine which, with practice, becomes
fairly automatic in play. Never treat any shot involving side
with a casual approach, indeed, real care is essential.

Let us start by striking a ball over the spots up the table
with side. Strike your ball to the side of centre, striking in
the normal way (not forgetting that smooth follow through and
ensuring that your bridge hand is very firm). Continue to play
the shot using left and right side alternatively, using maximum
side (striking further from the ball's centre) and lesser amounts,
making mental notes of your power of cueing.

Do not be tempted to dig into the shot. This is a common
failing, and it can play havoc with your shots. You must remember to push your cue through on the line and follow through,
trying to keep your cue on the bridge hand, since when side
is used, direction of the cue ball becomes less predictable. Therefore, smoothness in delivery is less likely to push the cue ball off
the line, whereas a jab in your cueing, when striking off centre,
is likely to have this very effect. This pushing off the line happens in varying degrees when side is applied, but when the shot
is played accurately the side pulls the ball back on line before
it strikes the object ball.

Side and the Nap

The amount of swerving you will find varies on different tables
according to the quality of the cloth and the amount of wear
it may have had. All billiard table cloth has a nap, and when
it is fastened to the table it is put on in such a way that the
nap travels from the baulk end to the spot end of the table. I
will discuss nap and its effects in detail later; just let us say
here that a strong nap will cause side and screw shots to react
with a liveliness and a sharpness of action which will soon make
you play every such shot with respect for it, and appreciate the

value of central striking. On the other hand, should you be playing on a table which has a bare cloth, almost devoid of any nap, you will find it will take more cue effort to make the side work on the bed of the table, and you will also find your plain ball shots will go through very accurately and very easily, to your satisfaction.

To delve into the more subtle uses of side at this stage would be premature, so let it suffice that the nap be accepted in principle for the moment. There is, however, one thing that should be stressed with regard to side whenever it is being used : that the pace of the shot is extremely important. If you play a fast shot the effect of the nap quite obviously will be far less. The speed of the ball will not give the nap the chance to work on it.

If the shot is played slowly, however, the nap will take effect and begin to pull the ball one way or the other, so pace judgment is important. If you have played the shot at an incorrect pace your calculations will be thrown out. Always take care to pace your side shots as well as you can and get your timing right. If you can learn to appreciate this pace factor (by constant practice and observation) side can assist your playing a lot. Of course the pace of a ball is also affected by the resilience of the cushions, if it strikes them, but in this case I am purely considering the basic pace of the bed of the table.

Remember that when you are potting an object ball, you will rarely be using a cushion first, therefore any side you are applying to your shot will be working on its way to the ball being potted. It is the pace over that distance that must be assessed correctly, in conjunction with the amount of side being used, and the type of cloth you are playing on. Such are the dangers when side is involved.

Practice Shots with Side
Thus far then, we have learnt that by striking the cue ball to the left or right of centre, giving it a sideways rotation, will change the natural direction of the cue ball. So you now have the power to alter the angle that the cue ball takes from the

object ball to its target by the application of side, in varying degrees, imparting either running side or check side, terms which are self explanatory.

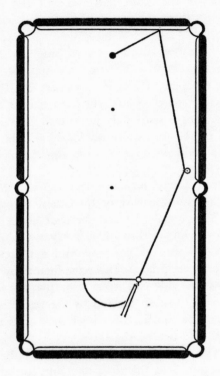

FIG 10.

As examples, let us consider three shots, cannon, a pot, and an in-off. Figure 10 illustrates a cannon from hand with the angle far too wide for a direct shot which means we are confronted with a one-cushion cannon. Without the use of side the cannon would still not be possible, so running side has to be applied. This will enable the cue ball to come off the top cushion at a more acute angle in the direction of the red ball on the spot. After a few attempts at a shot like this, you will become a little more aware of the accuracy that is demanded in the striking of the cue ball to ensure that you have put on the correct amount of side.

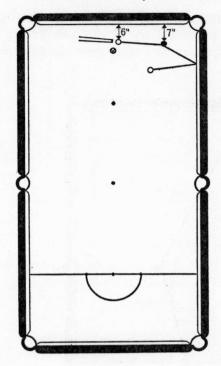

FIG 11.

Figure 11 shows the cue ball between the black, on its spot, and the top cushion, in a favourable position for potting a red. After doing so, you would want to get into position to pot the black. A plain ball shot in this case would allow the cue ball to drift too far down the table, leaving an angled pot on the black, which might well prove too difficult. So in potting the red, check side has to be applied, off the side cushion. This will bring the cue ball off the side cushion at a sharper angle and thus into line for a nice, easy black.

Figure 12 shows a set-up similar to the long loser shot described earlier. This time, though, there is a slight variation since the angle has been made a little wider, say 2 inches, by placing the cue ball on the corner spot of the 'D', making the angle too wide for a natural in-off.

Now you will find that by playing the shot in the usual way, but adding just a little running side, you will get the stroke quite easily. When practising, try playing this shot at varying paces, and you will see the effect that pace can have on a shot played with side.

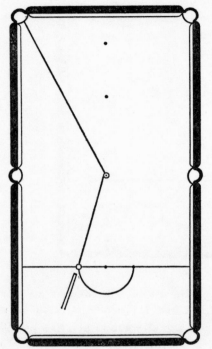

FIG 12.

The slow run-through losing hazard off the red, shown in Figure 13, is an extremely useful practice stroke which can vary in so many ways that you will not only find it beneficial to your cue action, timing and aiming, but also to understanding touch and control. The position of the red is tight on the top cushion, approximately 12 inches from the top right hand corner pocket, the white some 18 inches behind, 6 inches from the top cushion.

Now, by aiming for full ball contact on the red with slightly above centre striking with left-hand side on the cue ball, you will find that the red, when contacted, will make way for the

56

white to run through along the top cushion, spinning into the pocket off the far jaw. The general tendency with this shot is to over-hit in strength and lose control of the red ball. If you play the shot to make your cue ball just reach the pocket and fall in you will find that the red ball will always be in play in the centre of the table.

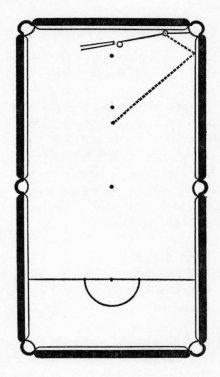

FIG 13.

As you become more proficient at this shot, move the red ball back in stages until you find you are able to get this shot with the red ball behind the billiard spot. Play the stroke at varying paces, controlling the speed of the cue ball along the cushion into the pocket, thereby putting varying pace into the red, or object, ball. When you are able to achieve this, you will find that your confidence will grow and so will your capabilities of assessing the strength of a shot. Do not forget to play this shot

57

the other side of the table also, into the opposite pocket, using correct side.

The follow through, and the striking of the cue ball just above the centre and to the side, are extremely important in this stroke. The follow through gives the nice free run of the ball along the cushion, and the top side which is applied to the ball persuades it to hug the top cushion.

The Screw Shot

Screw is another spinning effect placed upon the cue ball, causing it to recoil from the object ball at any desired angle, within certain bounds. I am not concerned here with freak shots, or even really very deep screw shots when the cue ball is several feet away from the object ball. You might well see a top player try a desperately hard screw shot the length of the table in the hope that it may come off and get him out of trouble, but you will invariably find that these shots are born of desperation rather than of choice. For our present purposes I am only interested in telling you how to perform a nicely executed screw shot without too much force and with a great deal of control.

Correct Stance and Wrist Action

One of the greatest and commonest mistakes made when playing any screw shot is lack of balance. Positioning of the body is important; there should be no movement at all on delivery of the stroke.

It is absolutely vital with a screw stroke that you strike low and that you hit where you meant to hit. Very often a player thinks that he actually struck the cue ball very low when, in fact, as he was going to play the shot there was a slight doubt in his mind and the cue tip tended to come up a little. Therefore, he would not get the deep screw action that he thought he should have.

This, when you think about it, is a deviation off the line of the shot. You must not funk the shot as you go through for fear, perhaps, of making the ball jump or tearing the cloth. So it is very important to keep the cue as near parallel to the table as you possibly can. By doing this you will be certain in your own mind that the cue will go right through the shot without any fear of touching the bed of the table. If you are confident about this before the shot is played, it will assist you very greatly in striking the ball where you meant to strike it.

There must be no holding back of the cue at all. The follow through has to be as complete and as full as in any other stroke. The only difference is that, on the moment of contact with the cue ball, the cue is given added impetus with a slight wrist action. This is done by momentarily releasing the grip, and re-gripping at the precise moment of impact with the cue ball. In my own case, I transfer the hold on my cue butt from the front of the hand to the back, retaining the grip with my little finger. This action allows the wrist to go forward, making the complete follow through possible, which is where the power comes from.

Many times I have heard it said that the cue should be gripped or squeezed as you strike, when playing the screw shot. I feel this can be misleading, because if the pressure is not released, the flow of the delivery becomes stunted, and the effect is a semi-stun shot. Hold your cue and try the action I have described, from the playing position. Just throw the cue butt with a wrist action from the forefinger hold, to a little finger hold, and note how your wrist comes forward, allowing you to make the complete follow through more easily.

Practice Screw Shots
Let us play a shot with screw between the two centre pockets, placing the red ball on the centre spot with the cue ball 12 inches behind, it, so that we are lined up for what looks like a six-shot into one centre pocket (Figure 14). Remember to keep the cue as low and as near parallel to the table as possible striking the cue ball with a nice crisp delivery, and on contact with the cue ball apply the wrist and grip action, and allow the follow through to continue to the end of its run.

You will find that, once you begin to get the timing of the stroke and the grip action at the right moment of delivery, you will begin to get this reaction of the cue ball coming back to you, even to the point where you may find that the cue ball returns so quickly that it comes into contact with the tip of your cue on the follow through. Do not worry about this; once you get to that stage of being able to bring the cue ball back in the desired manner you will find you will automatically move the cue from its path. Remember that by striking the red ball perfectly in the centre with the cue ball, the cue ball, with screw applied, will meet with greater resistance, which will give it added impetus on its return journey. It should not take you long to be able to pot the red and screw the cue ball back into the opposite centre pocket.

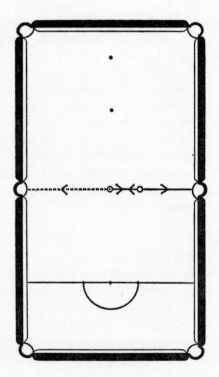

Fig 14.

One very common fault, when playing any screw shot, is that a player tends to raise his head on the shot and this takes away some of the power from the shot. You must make sure that you keep well down on the shot and go right through with the cue. If you have any difficulty with keeping the cue on the line of the shot, or find that the effort of the shot throws the cue from the hand, try the looped finger bridge illustrated earlier.

Having got the feel of this shot, you should now be beginning to feel pretty confident in your cueing and feeling the urge to press on, but let me give you a warning at this stage. When you are practising screw shots for any period of time you will find that your cueing may begin to become a little jerky. The best thing to do, then, is to go from your screw shot practice and return to a little red ball play, just pushing the cue through nicely, trying one or two run throughs along the cushion just to keep the freedom of the cue going. Never at any time neglect your practice with the red ball.

To continue with screw shots we now have to split or divide the object ball for positional purposes. To do this first take an imaginary line parallel to the baulk line, 16¾ inches below the middle spot; better still if you can mark the line very lightly with tailor's chalk (Figure 15). Then place the red ball on the centre spot and the cue ball 20 inches along that line from the side cushion. From this position you will now have a screw shot into the centre pocket to get the in-off by striking the red ball thin, or very thin, according to where you strike your cue ball. In fact, your contact on the red will be governed by the position you wish to leave this ball in, after having completed the stroke. Practise from this position a few times first, then try a range of strokes into either centre pocket from that line by moving the cue ball along the line until you are right behind the red, facing up the table. From this last position you have an in-off into either centre pocket, completely at right angles to you. This type of practice shot will be extremely helpful to the snooker player. Such control of screw and touch will often be called for when potting the blue ball off its spot, and trying to avoid other balls.

In this range of strokes you will find you are able to cover almost every variation of screw shot, varying strength of the

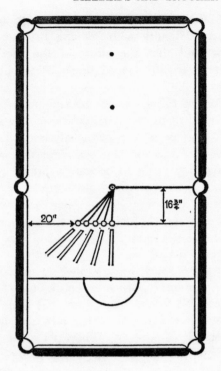

FIG 15.

shot, delicacy of touch, and thick or thin striking. Side should not be used in any of these shots. Remember these are pure screw shots, calling for low striking of the ball according to the amount of screw you feel is needed – which, of course, in turn will be governed by the thickness with which the object ball is being struck. This is a very testing but valuable practice sequence for players of all standards.

Screw Plus Side
To add side to screw shots for the billiard player is, in many respects, like adding a security measure to many of the shots that he can play. To appreciate this point, set up a shot at the top end of the table into either of the corner pockets by placing the red ball 18 inches from the top cushion and 1 inch from the side cushion with the cue ball parallel to it, say 12 inches

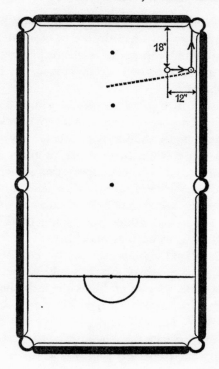

FIG 16.

from the side cushion (Figure 16), which means that you now have an in-off into the top corner pocket.

First of all I would like you to play the shot purely as a screw shot, that is with low striking and about half-ball contact. Try and screw into the top pocket 18 inches along the side cushion, with just the right amount of screw to take you gently into the pocket. I have no doubt you will find this rather difficult, because the shot demands accuracy of direction of the cue ball, and should you catch the first bump of the jaw you will find that the ball will just gently come off and hit the other jaw, wriggle in the opening of the pocket, and stay there.

Next, placing the balls back in the same position, play the shot with right-hand side, and screw, hitting the ball with a nice crisp stroke. You should find that the cue ball will take the same course along the cushion, and when it strikes the first jaw it will come off on to the second jaw and zip into the pocket. Of course, by now you will be aware of what degree of side to play on the shot, according to which top pocket you are playing it into. The shot we have just played would, of course, be into the right top pocket of the table.

If you were playing this type of shot in a game this would not be considered an easy one. You would give priority to getting the shot rather than thinking too accurately of position. But to take things a stage further, let us move the red ball closer to the pocket, say 9 inches from the corner pocket with the white parallel to it. We now have a similar shot but much closer to the pocket, which naturally makes the shot quite a lot easier, so we can also consider positioning of the object ball to make the next shot as easy as possible.

By playing with left-hand side, which in this case would be running side, you can make the object ball take a wider angle and come across the table off two cushions towards the middle pockets. If you play with check side – which would be right-hand side in this case – this will tend to keep the red ball straight across the table, to take up maybe just the position you require. The point is that from this shot you can see the possibility of maintaining a good position for your next shot. This, of course, presents a variety of shots in many parts of the table to which you can apply screw and side.

A warning about this particular shot though: when playing with left-hand side – the running side – should your ball bump into the jaw rather than going straight into the pocket, the left-hand side will have a neutralising effect against the jaw of the pocket, which, instead of pulling the ball in, will tend to hold it out. So with your running side shot you have to be very careful to make sure that you get a direct entry into the pocket.

To give you further practice in control and touch from this stroke, and to understand the use of running or check side a little more, gradually move the cue ball closer to the top cushion (Figure 17). This means that the further you get down the table, or closer to the top cushion, so the angle becomes such that you have to put more screw back into the shot. You will then see and really appreciate the use of check as opposed to running side. Quite obviously when you get into that sort of position you would never think of using the running side shot, but try it out, just to witness the effect.

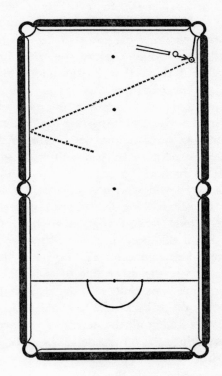

FIG 17.

To the advanced billiard player, this application of side to the cue ball, either running or check, can be of great advantage for positional purposes. The snooker player would be more discerning in his use of side, as his margin for error is far less. To attempt any potting with strong side, when the cue ball is more than 2 or 3 feet away from the object ball, is asking for trouble.

The Stun Shot

I consider the stun shot one of the most useful little shots on a billiard table. It is invaluable both to the snooker player and to the billiard player, particularly playing top of the table. I have heard it called the sledge-hammer shot, and the drive shot, terms which suggest that many people do not consider it calls for a great deal of thought or intelligence. In fact, it is a shot which demands as much skill and nicety of touch as any other shot.

It would be very easy to draw diagrams to demonstrate the many, many shots that one could play to use stun, in either billiards or snooker. But I think that if you understand how to get the desired effect for stun, the drawing of various positions really is not necessary. It is more a question of practising correct execution of stroke and imparting the desired effect to the cue ball. If you can perform this with certainty for one particular shot there is no reason why you cannot do so whenever the position calls for such action.

The shot I have selected will serve the purpose for billiards and snooker. Place the red ball on the billiard spot and the white ball 13 inches behind it and 16½ inches from the top cushion (Figure 18). From this position you will see we have a slightly angled pot into the top pocket. The object of the exercise is to get the cue ball to the other side of the red position into any of the dozen positions that you might wish to take up for further play. You do so by potting the red with a fairly crisp and firm stroke, but killing all the action of your cue ball, so that it just goes through to the other side of the red's position at the angle you desire.

Let us say that we want to get the white ball into position for a pot into the opposing pocket at the top of the table. By striking your ball just below centre and gripping your cue a little tighter you should pot the red and hardly go through at all with the cue on the delivery. In your first attempts at this you may find that you are screwing the cue ball back. In this case make sure you are not striking the cue ball too low; remember you want to strike just below centre, with very little follow through on the shot, and you should be gripping the cue a little tighter than normal. The red ball contact is full-face.

You will find that the sharper you strike the ball the more

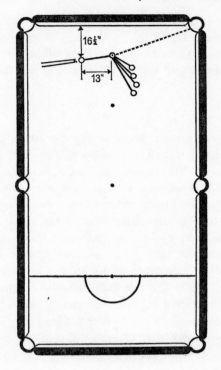

FIG 18.

acute an angle you can squeeze from the red, to bring your cue ball further down the table. The shot has to be played freely, and once you begin to get the feel of it you will be surprised at the power with which you can play the shot to make your own ball travel just a few inches. Bear in mind that this is plain ball striking; use no side whatsoever. With practice, you will find it quite possible to get a series of winning hazards from the spot starting from this position, without touching either of the side cushions at all. Once you have got to this stage you will find that these stun shots will be cropping up at different times during your game, and you will find yourself playing stun run throughs for cannons, pots or in-offs, whether they be almost power shots or fairly delicate strokes.

To make the cue ball stop dead on contact with the object ball, fractionally lower striking has to be made. You will find

67

as the cue ball gets further away from the object ball slightly lower striking is needed. The stun run through at long range becomes a more difficult shot, but is quite possible, demanding greater all-round control and timing of stroke; it is a shot more for the expert.

The Drag Shot

A habit which players should avoid is playing for a pot at a slow pace, striking the cue ball so weakly that it only has just enough strength to reach the object ball and push it gently into the pocket. The danger of this is that you are allowing the cue ball and the object ball to be affected by any unevenness of table, the effect of nap (more about this in the next chapter) and so on. In cases where the cue ball may have to travel perhaps the length of the table you can apply what is called drag to the cue ball to slow it initially to the required pace. To do this you must strike the cue ball below the centre, very crisply, causing it to revolve in a reverse action as opposed to the usual action when a ball is rolling forward. This has the effect of imparting what is virtually a skid effect on the cue ball, still keeping it dead on line (assuming that you struck centrally). Only when this reverse action ceases to have effect will the ball begin to roll in the normal forward motion.

This drag effect can be applied to the cue ball with a good deal of accuracy. You will find that you are able to play such shots with great control over the cue ball. Play the shot firmly and your ball will literally skid for perhaps four or five feet, then, having lost its reverse action, it will begin to roll forward at a slower pace, having lost its power and having covered most of the journey to the object ball. Therefore, you have played the stroke at the strength required, but have overcome any effects of roll on the table, nap, and so on. Yes, drag is an extremely useful shot, though I must add that it is more for the advanced player than the beginner.

CHAPTER EIGHT

Billiard Cloth and Nap

A billiard cloth has a right and a wrong side. The right side, as far as we are concerned, is the side that has the nap, and when the cloth is placed on the table it is the nap which is uppermost. The nap has to run from the baulk end to the top end of the table, so whenever the table is brushed and ironed it has to be brushed from the baulk end up to the spot end and then ironed from the baulk to the spot end. This is most important and it should never be done in any other way.

It is quite likely that you will come across billiard tables where the nap is not uppermost. Many clubs and billiard halls find, that, due to the heavy cost of recovering a table, they can only afford to turn the cloth when it shows signs of wear or is completely worn, so they merely turn the cloth over. Thus the expression arises 'playing on a turned cloth'. In such cases you are playing on the side of the cloth which has virtually no nap at all, and therefore the reaction that you get when you are playing may differ a good deal from the normal. I can only advise you to avoid such tables when possible.

As in all things, quality varies. You will find that with a good quality cloth there is a silky feel when you run your hand with the nap and you will be surprised by the strong resistance there is to your hand, when you press it gently against the nap. Of course, the newer the cloth, or the better the quality, the more noticeable will be the nap reaction on side. So while you are learning, and using every game to practice the many aspects of stroke play we have discussed thus far, it is better to get as near to ideal conditions as possible, so that you are not puzzled by factors not due to your playing.

Effects of Side Play with and against the Nap

If we were applying left-hand side, which means striking to the left of the cue ball, there would be a slight pushing off from the line it would take, towards the right. The amount that the cue ball is pushed off the line will naturally vary according to the power of the shot, but, playing with the nap, the effect will be for the nap to pull the cue ball back on to the line by the time it has reached its object. Of course, that is a simplification of matters. Varying thicknesses of nap will have different effects. A thick heavy nap will pull far more than a fine or smooth nap. To just what degree only experience will tell you, but as a rule you must remember that, when striking to the left of centre, the cue ball is pushed slightly off to the right, and striking to the right the cue ball is pushed slightly to the left – and, of course, that this amount of swerve is governed by the strength that is put into the stroke and the distance the cue ball has to travel. Reaction on the cue ball from nap when side is applied is best observed when the cue ball, still spinning, is beginning to travel slowly. You will then see it curl on the nap of the cloth, according to the degree of side that you have applied.

Playing against the nap, however, the effect of side is altered. Assume that we are striking to the left of the cue ball and we are facing from the spot end of the table striking down towards the baulk end. If we applied left-hand side we would still get the same slight push off to the right, but, in this case, with the nap being in the reverse direction, instead of pulling the cue ball back on to line, it tends to let the cue ball drift in the direction of the throw off. In other words, instead of pulling to the left it will pull to the right, which, of course, is almost a complete reversal of the action as played with the nap.

Now if you want to demonstrate this for yourself, place a red ball over the corner pocket in the baulk end and put the cue ball by the top pocket at the spot end, on the same side of the table. If you play to pot the ball in the baulk pocket you will find that by playing with left-hand side to hit the ball into the pocket your cue ball will drift to the right, completely missing the object ball (Figure 19.) This assumes, of course, that the shot is played at a pace at which the nap can work on the cue ball, and, of course if you use right-hand side and play to miss, the reverse will apply; the cue ball will pull into the object ball and knock it into the pocket. So you see that by playing left-hand side the ball pulls to the right, and by playing right-hand side, away from the object ball, it will pull to the left and pot this ball.

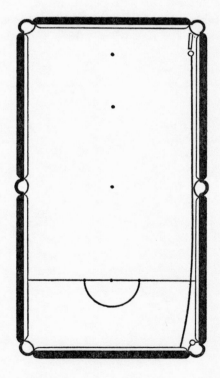

Fig 19.

From this explanation, you can appreciate, when striking a long ball down the table against the nap, just how it can pull your cue ball one way or the other should you strike a little to left or right instead of centrally. You may have heard players remark that the table rolls one way or the other. They are probably wrong, misinterpreting what is happening when shots are being played at a strength which allows the nap to work. The player is quite unaware that the cue ball has been struck lightly to one side or the other, so the ball is being pulled off the line of the shot. Of course, the skilled player can take subtle advantage of this very effect, but I would advise the average player, when playing against the nap, to play the shot at a strength which will overcome its effect on the cue ball, to play with central striking, and aim as accurately as the shot demands. To try applying side against the nap can be asking for trouble. Playing across the table, that is across the nap, there is little or no effect at all on the cue ball when side is applied.

CHAPTER NINE

The Art of Potting

The pot is the most difficult shot, as far as accuracy is concerned, that one can play on a billiard table. In billiards it is vitally essential to master potting if you aspire to being adept at top-of-the-table play, which is synonymous with being a first-class billiard player. To be a snooker player of any class at all, demands accuracy and cueing power of the highest order.

Point of Aim

Theorising on the subject of potting is difficult, but somehow showing a player how to pot does not convey the message alone. He really needs some acquaintance with basic potting theory if he is to grasp the practice.

To start with, let us establish what some correct lines of aim are: place a ball on the centre spot and from the middle of the centre pocket draw a line through the centre of that ball, to a point facing the other pocket (Figure 20). You now have the exact point of aim for potting the ball back along that line into the pocket. If you should put your cue ball anywhere on the table where you can strike that point on the object ball with the cue ball, you will be able to pot the ball from that spot into the centre pocket.

This principle is rather easier to establish than to carry out. I find it most difficult to find a spot so small on an object ball where I can say with confidence that is where I have to strike with my cue ball, and so do most players. I cannot

73

think of many things more difficult than judging accurately and consistently the contact point of two spheres.

In truth, most players in the early stages take potting very much for granted. They only begin to reason how to do it as they gain ability and are striving to do better. To demonstrate ways towards potting improvement, I have to make an assumption – a reasonable one if you have followed through in your practice the earlier lessons in this book – that you have a good cue action.

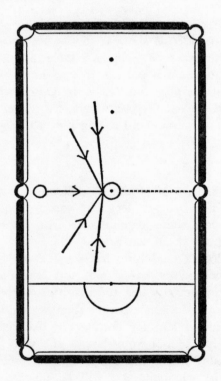

FIG 20.

Recognition of Angles

If I put a ball on the centre spot and place the cue ball for a very simple straight pot into the centre pocket, I have little doubt that if I asked a dozen players with a decent cue action to pot the ball into the centre pocket they would all do this without difficulty. They would do so because they could look at the shot and recognise the angle immediately. In such a case they could hardly do otherwise.

If I moved the cue ball 18 inches to the left or to the right to give quite an acute-angled pot probably only one out of the twelve would get the pot with any consistency. That would be because the successful one recognises the angle as easily as all the others recognised the first direct one. The other eleven players need practice at that pot to imprint on their minds the angle of that shot. Once learned, they should be able to pot it more regularly; they have another shot in their mental locker.

This mental recognition of the angle that the object ball travels to the pocket, and the angle of the cue ball to the object ball, is the essence of good potting. When you have established the line of aim, you just have to deliver the cue along that line. Such confidence comes mainly through gradually studied play, building up acquaintance with more and more angles. You must appreciate that the object ball is struck half-way nearer to its centre than the line of aim that is made with the cue, except in full-ball contacts (see Figure 21).

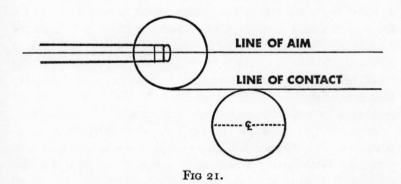

FIG 21.

The only points of aim on the object ball to which you can truly claim to have a visual point at which to aim are the full-ball contact and the half-ball aim, the latter being

75

when the centre of your cue is aimed through the centre of the cue ball to the edge of the object ball. A third point is when you are playing at the extreme edge of the object ball for a thin shot. Now this does not mean to say that every other sort of pot is completely unpredictable. Obviously the more you play various tricky angled shots, the greater the chance you have at pulling them off.

It is because it is so difficult to find this vital spot of aim on a ball that the game of snooker is so competitive. My own method of practice has been to establish as many familiar potting angles at half-ball and quarter-ball aiming as possible, and then practise them until they become pretty sure shots. I find that anything in between these points, or in close proximity to them, begins to become easier to recognise and play.

Practising a Range of Angles

This can best be done in systematic fashion, by lining up the fullest possible range of potting angles in practice. These are shown in Figure 22.

Using the top half of the table, with an imaginary line drawn between the centre pockets, the pink ball is placed on its spot. By placing a ball over the centre pocket, you have a full-ball aim on the pink into the corner pocket. A ball placed directly opposite the pink, on the side cushion, will give a quarter-ball aim into the corner or centre pockets, on the other side of the table. Two more balls are spaced equally between, giving you a three-quarter-ball aim into the corner pocket and a half-ball aim into the same pocket.

Pursuing this principle further, by simulating these positions around the other top end cushions, it can be seen how you may familiarise yourself with a variety of shots by this method. It is easier to make mental notes when you can see all the lines of aim drawn in as on the diagram.

For practice purposes move the cue ball in on the line of aim from the cushion until you can form a good bridge hand to play the shots, then move back towards the cushions as you progress. This method will imprint on your mind the majority of angled pots required, and will test your technique to the full.

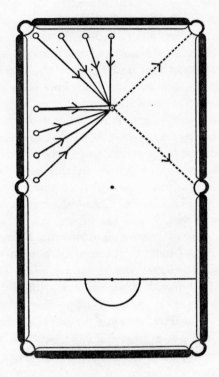

Fig 22.

I think perhaps I should emphasise, in showing these half-ball, quarter-ball and three-quarter-ball shots that the aiming must be taken with the cue on the line of the shot, aiming the tip of the cue at a particular part of the object ball. That is to say that when playing your half-ball, you must aim through the centre of the cue ball to the edge of the object ball. Of course, with a quarter-ball aim you will find that you have to aim the tip of your cue off the edge of the object ball which, of course, does make the shot a little chancy, to say the least, bearing in mind the accuracy required in contact, but the individual will gradually get accustomed to his own

77

sighting and recognise what he must do to pull off a given shot.

The three-quarter-ball aim is made by aiming your cue through the centre of the cue ball at the quarter section of the object ball, appropriate to the direction in which you wish to send it. Once you begin to find the correct aim to get a given pot, practise this one again and again to imprint it on your memory, but never be discouraged on the occasions you miss a pot that you thought you had mastered; remember that guarantee of a certain contact is quite impossible – this is what makes the game so attractive.

It is not until you really get down to potting that you begin to appreciate the accuracy that is needed and just what a tiny part of the ball has to be struck to get the desired effect, and it is for this reason that nowhere in this book will you find me referring to a contact. You will note that all the time we are taking points of aim, on the line of the stroke, and not on points of contact. In fact, if you are taking just an ordinary half-ball aim, your point of contact is different. Therefore, to keep referring from a half-ball or quarter-ball aim to quarter-ball contact or half-ball contact would only confuse the issue and would have a detrimental effect on one's play.

After persistent practice at these fixed-position shots, you should find that, as you develop some mastery of them, the in-between positions will not appear difficult; you will fall into line with them almost straight away. This set-position potting routine can be practised in other parts of the table. Practise the quarter-ball aim particularly; this is not quite so easily stored in your shots-memory as the half-ball, but with much practice you should be able to get it as consistently as the half-ball.

Potting Concentration

Once you have taken aim, the concentration on the imaginary line has to be very strong. This is most important. One of the things that contributes to the difficulty of potting is being surrounded by other balls which tends to distract you from the job in hand, and this is where the determination comes in. Once you have got down, taken your aim and committed yourself in your sighting you must then apply all your concentration to delivering the cue. Logically the success of the shot is a natural sequel to sure aiming and good delivery. What follows is just a question of playing the shot at the correct strength. You should be able to concentrate on good positioning for the subsequent shot. I quite appreciate that what we are saying is pure theory, but I believe that if you understand the theory and try hard to apply it you will succeed.

Remember to keep your cueing smooth when you are playing these shots. In your preliminary cue motions backwards and forwards, play at a nice even tempo, and when you finally make the delivery make it at the same tempo. Do not suddenly throw the cue forward at faster speed but try and keep everything even. Remember that at the moment of contact your eyes must be glued on to the object ball on the line of aim. Timing is the other important factor, which we have already discussed.

Make sure that you do not raise your head or move your head at all on the stroke. When you have completed the delivery, remain in position and do not move until you have seen the result of your shot.

I would like to make it quite clear that, although I have said I like to find as many spots on the table from where the half ball can be played for practice purposes, I do not advocate that everybody should try and remember all these places and use them as a blueprint for their play. These pots, wherever they may be, are purely for practice purposes, though of course, when you are playing you may find you are close to the line subtended by one of these spots, so familiarity will breed confidence.

Addressing Correctly

On occasions, when I have been discussing the different ways and approaches of various players to how they take aim and address the ball, I have been told, and noticed, that they find it difficult to find the centre of the cue ball when they are addressing. Therefore they dip their cue and do their pre-delivery strokes while addressing the cue ball right at the bottom. Here, where the ball meets the table, there is less margin for error, but on the final delivery, of course, you have to raise your cue as you go through to strike the part that you wish to. My own experience is that this is very difficult to do successfully, so I would advise any player starting from scratch, who wants to develop good style, to learn to aim correctly in the first place. In other words, he should take his aim and his preamble into the shot by addressing the ball where he means to strike it. Potting is hard enough without adding extra complications, like needing to raise the tip of the cue as you come through on the final stroke.

CHAPTER TEN

Half-ball Potting Practice

For further practice in judging half-ball potting angles I advocate sessions potting the colours from their spots from a variety of positions. It is an interesting exercise, which naturally relates closely to actual play, while impressing again on the mind the various angles likely to be met with frequently.

Potting the Colours
Reference marks are made on the cushions, but again you should give yourself a chance to cue freely at first by moving the cue ball along the line of aim, enabling a sound bridge to be made. The advanced player can cue from the cushion; it is important to master this eventually, as it is always an awkward position in a game. You will find the head tends to come up on this type of stroke more than on most, purely because of the inward tension felt from being tucked up on the cushion.

A very useful angle to remember for potting the black from its spot, is to mark a spot $7\frac{3}{4}$ inches down the side cushion from the top cushion (see Figure 23). The line from this point on the side cushion to the black spot will give you the half-ball aim into either of the corner pockets, depending on which side of the table you are playing.

To pot the green, a mark 7 inches inside the baulk line on the side cushion will give you the half-ball aim into the middle pocket. This naturally applies to the equivalent position on the other side of the table for the yellow.

To pot the brown into the middle pocket, mark a spot 15 inches inside the baulk line either side of the table, lines up for half ball aim for the middle pockets. To pot the brown into the corner pockets (the baulk pockets), a spot 10 inches outside the baulk line either side of the table will give you the correct line. For potting the blue into the centre pocket the half-ball aim is 18 inches on the side cushion, either side of the centre pocket.

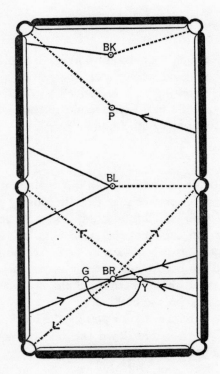

Fig 23.

Do not forget that for any of these pots when you are going against the nap of the cloth – that is when you are potting down the table – the strength has to be played at a pace that will overcome the effect of the nap on the object ball (assuming, of course, that it has a fair distance to travel). Additionally, if the cue ball has a fair distance to travel before it reaches the object ball it must be played at a pace that will not allow the nap to pull it slightly off course.

A little practice will soon allow you to appreciate these points. For instance, if you play at a fairly gentle pace to pot the pink from its spot into the centre pocket, from a point somewhere behind the pink towards the top corner pocket, you should always play to the far jaw of the pocket. This will allow any pull by the nap that is effected on the object ball to draw it into the centre of the pocket. If you aim to the near jaw you will find that you will probably pull further into the cushion and miss the pocket completely. In fact, by aiming to the further jaw this can give you quite a large pocket area to aim for.

At this stage, we have covered a great deal of ground. If the reader has taken his practice in the sequence of this book, he should have had some idea about scheming his method of play, and if his ability has kept pace with his acquisition of knowledge, then he should be doing very well.

It may appear that not a great deal has been said about potting in general terms for snooker. Though books of diagrams and explanations might well analyse a number of situations, the true requirement is increased ability, and this is what I have mainly been intent on teaching. However, Figure 23 does a useful job in making many potting points a little clearer, the lines drawn from cushion to ball indicating the half-ball aiming for the colours on their spots.

At first glance this particular diagram might appear just a conglomeration of lines and perhaps a little baffling. I am not in favour of too much shot-analysis diagram drawing, but this illustrates some very valid points. When you appreciate that anywhere along those lines you can put the cue ball and a pot will be on with one ball or another you will have some indication of the tremendous range of shots that will be within your compass if you master these set shots, not just from the cushion but from various places along the line. You can then diversify by applying your ability to use side, screw and stun to your potting, where these forms of control may be appropriate.

These set potting positions give another fine chance to check on your stance, cue delivery and timing of the stroke. When you play a shot successfully and you feel that everything has gone correctly, note the position of the cue ball when it comes to rest, then repeat the shot several more times and just see how accurately you can get the cue ball to the same position. This will give you an indication of your consistency in striking.

Do try at all times to keep your practising interesting. Once you feel that you are losing a little interest or getting slightly bored by continued repetition of one particular stroke, leave it alone and turn to something else to keep your interest alive. When you begin to lose enthusiasm for a particular part of the game you will find that the concentration goes and you do not benefit. I have always found it good practice to pot all the colours off their spots, starting each time from a different position. When I am really in the mood, I will try to pot the colours off their spots, but after potting each colour, I mark where the cue ball has stopped; then, having cleared the colours, I start again from the same spot and see how accurately I can play to the same positions for the next series. This sort of thing keeps you on your mettle, and of course, improves your positional play.

Another set exercise that I have always found easy to hold interest, is, with the colours on their spots, to put four reds between the black and the pink (Figure 24). Then try to pot red, black, red, black, four times. I endeavour to get down on to the yellow off the last black, then try to take the colours.

This, of course, would give you a nice break and at the same time allow you to familiarise yourself with all the various angles of potting. Of course, to play these set pieces well, with any consistency, you would have to be a good player.

I would think that for the average snooker player, the blue is the favourite ball, for the reason that it is in the open part of the table and quite close to the centre pockets, which makes it very inviting. The important thing when playing to get on the blue is to pay a great deal of importance to strength to see if you can, if possible, get on the right side of the blue, which will enable you to pot it and run on to your next red more easily.

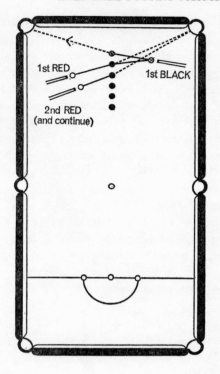

1st RED

1st BLACK

2nd RED
(and continue)

FIG 24.

Just the slightest angle is needed for this. Should you go just the wrong side of the blue, above or below, the hazards involved in getting your cue ball back into position can necessitate the use of side or missing the baulk-end colours and corner pockets.

I am often asked by various students of the game questions like: 'Am I seeing the angles right? I find I see some shots better than others.' If you have any doubts regarding your vision, you should see an oculist at an early stage, just to find if you have a correction in one eye as opposed to the other. This can make a difference to your playing, but you might well adapt to it quite happily. If, when you start playing, you grow accustomed to sighting the balls and getting the general picture with your eyesight as it is, you will doubtless find that you can manage quite well. But later, looking for improvement you might consult an oculist and be told that you need a correction in one eye. This, incidentally, is nothing to worry about, as it is quite common. However, if you then start trying to play with spectacles after a long period of having played without them you will find it very difficult to adjust. The correction which is applied to your weaker eye will upset your aiming, assessment and everything else, so if you decide to take up the game seriously, make a good start by seeing that your eyes are as they should be and, if not, start playing with spectacles. There is no more difference in playing with or without spectacles than there is with having to use them to read.

A short-range Advanced Shot

I have made it quite clear that side can be a dangerous thing to use when potting, and advise plain striking as much as possible. However, as progress is made and you become more

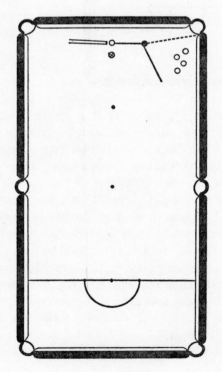

FIG 25.

expert, there will be times when side can be an asset as long as care is taken. Figure 25 is a very good example and a most useful shot to have in your locker. The principle can be applied in many ways, as long as you are reasonably close to the object ball. The position shows a red ball to be potted, with an easy black to follow, but in potting the red you cannot avoid other balls on the side cushions, which may spoil your chances on the black, and a plain stun shot is not on. By striking your cue ball to the right and below centre and taking your line of aim to about one inch to the right of the corner pocket, you will find that the cue ball will be deflected to the left, sending the object ball to the centre of the pocket, and the cue ball will stun screw to a position behind the black. A little practice at this shot will give you some indication of what you can do, and just how, more or less, cue power will do what is necessary.

What actually happens, if you study the shot, is this; your contact on the red is made fuller, which gives more resistance to the cue ball, enabling the stun screw effect to work, which, at the same time deflects the red off the line of aim into the pocket. One has to be a confident player to play this type of shot, and it should be remembered to play it only when necessary, and when you are able to judge to a fine limit the throw off you can apply to the object ball.

CHAPTER ELEVEN

Posture and Style Faults

A very common fault when using the rest is shown in plate 18. The player is obviously over-reached and, having struck the ball, is extended to the limit, which means that his poise and balance are non-existent. In such a case it would be far better to use the half butt and stand back from the table just a little so that you are able to play the stroke comfortably, and well within your reach. It is just as important when you have to reach out well over the table, resting your body on it and be as comfortable as when you are playing from a more normal position.

Many shots, though they do not need a rest, call for leaning over the table to get a good view of the line of aim. A common fault is to lean over half-heartedly, just cocking the head over. This incorrect position for such a shot is shown in plate 19.

Notice how, because the body is not behind the shot, the elbow has fallen out of line, and the wrist has become crooked on the stroke, putting the player in an awkward position for cueing. With the accuracy that is demanded for potting this could be enough to cause you to miss the shot and lose the frame.

Plate 20 shows this shot being played correctly. This time I have got my right leg up on to the table, resting the frame of my body vertically on it. I have got into a sound and strong position here, with my head well behind the shot. Notice how my elbow is in the correct position, the cueing is nice and parallel to the table and everything looks right. Such important points should not be neglected in a moment of haste, perhaps through excitement in being on the winning shot. Take your time and prepare yourself properly before executing the stroke.

Plate 21 shows a bad position of the cueing arm. Note how the arm from the shoulder to the elbow is quite off the line of aim and the wrist is cocked, holding the cue on a different line of aim other than the true one. It really is important to get that arm nicely lined up in a vertical position. You can see how pushing the cue through from this shot, with everything being out of line, would make everything difficult and give you a somewhat shaky cue delivery.

At first glance the position looks very good, very sound and solid. In fact, you might well get fair results adopting such a position. This is a common style used by some very good players but that does not mean to say there is no room for improvement. You want to straighten the elbow out a little on to the line and also that bend in the wrist. Hold the cue nicely in the hand with a dropped wrist rather than the cocked wrist shown. Such minor points may not hinder you but are worth ironing out – as they have been in the position shown in plate 22.

You might think the position shown in plate 23 is a reasonably good one. But the feet are too close together, and both legs are perfectly straight, which means that balance is not good by any standards, particularly if you should be playing a forcing stroke. If balance is bad when playing a forcing stroke, you shake the body and this causes a slight deviation of your cue; therein lies the fault. Note how the grip on the cue, while a light one, is just with the tips of the fingers. This is not the best of grips. Note also how the wrist is not in line with the rest of the forearm to the elbow. So many points of this position are at fault.

In plate 24 we have the correct style, the style which we are hoping to achieve; everything is nice and straight, and in line. This is generally a sound and solid-looking style, aiming is straight through the centre of the cue.

When you are playing or practising ask your partner to watch you. In fact, you can help one another by watching, explaining and correcting. It is very difficult to try to observe your own faults, and if you have somebody to help you, you can make the necessary corrections much quicker.

I can remember when I used to look in a dress table mirror with my hand on two or three books, to bring it to the correct height of a billiard table. I would spend hours looking in the mirror, addressing a ball to see if my cueing was accurate. The dressing table had two wing mirrors, a most useful feature, as I was able to observe myself from various angles and study all the points. I found this most helpful.

CHAPTER TWELVE

Tactics and Safety Play

Tactics, of course, play an extremely important part in both billiards and snooker. To start with, the best advice I can offer is that, before you get down on your stroke, you must make up your mind whether you intend to play for a pot or make a safety stroke. If it is to be a pot, decide whether it is possible to get good position for the subsequent shot or whether it is a pot to nothing. If you intend to play a safety shot, make sure it is a good one. There is nothing worse than getting down to play a pot and then, while you are down, changing your mind, playing a half-hearted shot with the hope that if you miss, it will go safe. If you are in a tight spot where you have been left in an awkward position you must get down with all the determination in the world and play the pot regardless of anything else, if you have decided on that course.

Tactics, naturally, play a very important part in snooker. The chap who has a good knowledge of angles and the cushions of a table will have a decided advantage, so it is as well to build up such knowledge as soon as possible.

A ball, played at a normal pace on to a cushion, will always take the same angle at which it was played when it leaves the cushion. As a practical example, suppose your cue ball was over the centre pocket and you wanted to pot a ball which was over the top pocket on the same side as your cue ball (Figure 26). By selecting a point of aim in the centre of the opposite cushion between the top pocket and centre pocket, you only need to play at normal pace to get the pot. The angles in this case are equal.

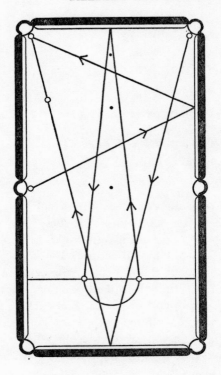

Fig 26.

If, however, you tried to force the cue ball on to the opposing cushion to get the same effect, you would find that, by doing this, you will distort the rubber. This throws the cue ball away at a different angle. The term is that the rubber is squeezed. You should remember that when playing such shots, they should be played at the normal pace for the table, otherwise this distortion takes place, producing a completely foreign angle of rebound.

A similar example of equal strike/rebound angles can be observed by placing the cue ball on the yellow spot and playing it up the table to strike the centre of the top cushion, directly behind the billiard spot. You will find that the cue ball will return down the table to the green spot.

One could illustrate diagrammatically thousands of positions where shots can be played for snookers, safety shots, and so on, but, I think such theory play is superfluous. Once a player has got a good working knowledge of the table, and has a fair under-standing of the angles and the degree of side that he can put on the cue ball, then he can assess a shot well enough; according to his own capabilities; he will know what he can go for. Much more important, I think, when playing for safety and to obtain snookers is, once again, to ensure that you play the shot with faultless technique – cueing, stance, staying still on the stroke, a good delivery, pace of the shot – are the important things. Seeing the angle is not the difficult part. It is more a question of delivering properly. Another important thing is to go round to the object ball and have a look from the other end of the shot, to make sure that you are not deceived from the cue end as to the angle that has to be taken from the object ball to the cushion going round another ball to give clearance, so that, perhaps, you get back to baulk again.

A common fault I have noticed amongst club players when they are playing the type of safety shot which is the long ball that has to be clipped so that the cue ball returns to baulk, is that they tend to raise their head on the stroke. This is because the cue ball has a long way to travel, so there is this tendency to lift the head at the crucial moment, as if to check up on the object-ball position again. It is most important to stay down on the stroke until you see the result of the shot. You will find then that your contacts on the object ball will be as intended.

To return to the potting of balls for a moment, I am sure now, having read thus far, that you will appreciate why we have stressed the importance of the stance and technique so much. You will perhaps still be mystified when at times you put a perfectly straight pot on the table and find that with all the best intentions, it still goes awry. Even a full-ball contact, so easily recognisable, can still be missed. This underlines the fact that you can never relax and take a shot for granted. The point of contact between the two balls is so small that you should concentrate hard at every shot.

I find it hard to lay down a system of play for snooker. It is a constantly changing game, one must play each stroke on its merit. Having decided what to play, whether it be a safety shot or snooker, a pot, or a shot to nothing, get down and play with control. As these things improve, so will your game.

One thing I have observed with monotonous regularity, which rather proves the point, is the break at snooker, which can so often be the reason for losing. The popular way is to come off the top red of the triangle with strong running side, to cross the table between the pink and blue, then on to the bottom cushion; a fine break. For the average club player or newcomer to the game, I consider this a dangerous shot for this reason. Here we are at the commencement of a match, maybe tensed up a little, and the first stroke you attempt to play is at a ball 9 feet away, needing bundles of side. I would suggest a plain ball stroke off the same red, spotting your cue ball close to the yellow, aiming for thinnish contact to come down off the side cushion, to the bottom cushion. Build yourself up to the more professional shot.

Billiards is a different game entirely, one where series of repetitious play can be made to great advantage, such as runs of losing hazards, or both winners and losers together. Linked with cannon play this is the main theme of amateur play; it's a wonderful game.

For the expert, top of the table play is a never-ending phase of play, demanding the highest skills of all, controlling three balls at one stroke, being able to improvise and using subtleties of stroke play, only evident to the player concerned, and possibly the expert spectator. However good you may get, there is still scope to go further.

The variation of strokes around the table are never-ending. The new rule, making a miss a foul stroke, was brought in to speed the game up a little, and to stop some of the time wasting and deliberations that can spoil a game. It is a rule with which I agree. It now makes safety play a more skilful business, compelling the player to strike a ball in doing so. The rule says:
Rule 8
A miss is a foul shot, except when the striker is in hand, and there is no ball out of baulk.

I think billiards is more demanding in terms of temperament.

Long sessions of waiting have to be endured, and the further a player gets behind, the more confident his opponent becomes, which does not help a worsening situation. At snooker, a frame lost means a fresh start. This is debatable but I think the point is valid. But really both games are complimentary to each other, and whichever you play, enjoyment should be the first and last consideration.

CHAPTER THIRTEEN

Constructive Cannon Play

For the average billiard player, a cannon – caused when the cue ball strikes the opponent's ball and the red ball, or vice versa – is invariably a link shot between a succession of losing hazards or winning hazards. Rarely do you find a succession of cannons being played. This phase of the game seems to be reserved for the very few players who are able to control close cannon play. Nonetheless, cannon play is undoubtedly a very important part of billiards, as indeed, it is of snooker, and has to be played very accurately indeed to serve its purpose. The important thing is the contact on the second object ball, which invariably turns out to be the important ball in cannon play.

Once you start to get involved with cannons, it should be remembered that for the first time, a player is beginning to try to control three balls instead of two. So, therefore, your contacts on the two object balls are vital.

Learning to Judge Cannon Contacts

To understand better the sort of contact that has to be made on the first and second object balls to get the required position, practise the cannon shot as set up in Figure 27. By playing a thick half ball on the first object ball, the red, the cue ball will reach the second object ball and keep it trapped on the cushion by making a full contact. The first object ball will then strike the side cushion nearest it and cross over to the other side cushion, coming to rest in close proximity to the top pocket. This shot would enable the continuance of either top of the table play (which I shall discuss in more detail later), or, if preferred, a delicate pot into the top pocket, leaving the white on the line for the cross loser to continue red ball play.

This sort of shot can be practised by making a mark on the

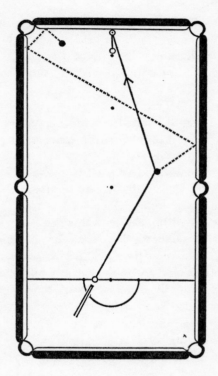

FIG 27.

table and placing the first object ball on it. Put the second object ball in position and persist in playing this several times, either side of the table, to impress the angle on your mind. You will find that as this angle varies in the play during a game, you will gradually accommodate as you do in a pot, and you will soon begin to assess correctly the right sort of contacts to get the desired results.

This shot should be played without any side at all and the cue must be pushed through on the stroke. This is vital. Make sure, too, that your delivery and timing are good. The effect on the cue ball should be that you rather tend to float the cue ball down the table, to the second object ball rather than letting it run freely. It should be a very precisely timed stroke indeed, and when you play it well the impression of control that it gives you will be very pleasing.

Any unintentional side that is put on the cue ball in this stroke can be disastrous. You might still get the cannon, but losing position could very well mean the end of the break. Do not forget to play this shot from both sides of the table.

The Vital First Contact

The most important thing to remember with this type of cannon, which is very similar to a drop cannon, is concentration on the first contact. When you have set your cue ball into position, having taken aim and committed yourself to the shot, keep your eyes fixed on the first object ball. It has been my experience when coaching to note so many players have trouble getting this type of shot or the drop cannon, through allowing their attention to wander. No sooner do they strike the cue ball, having taken their aim and decided on the thickness of their contact on the first object ball, they tend to let their eyes wander anxiously to the second object ball, in anticipation of the contact they are going to make with it. By so doing there is the tendency to let the cue follow the eyes, thus encouraging the player to allow the cue to go slightly off line.

I feel so strongly about getting this first contact right with drop cannon play, that I maintain it should be your primary aim to achieve this. Do not worry about the scoring of the shot, because you have committed yourself to the stroke, just have the courage to play exactly where you aim, accepting the fact that the rest will follow suit, if you have correct contact on the first object ball, and play the shot at correct strength.

The Second Ball Contact

After coping confidently with accurate first contact, you have more opportunity to concentrate on the strength of the shot. As your game improves, you will appreciate that it is the second

ball contact in cannon play which is so important to subsequent play. In fact, one of the secrets of the success of the
better player is that he is able to push the second object ball
just where he wants it, to make the following stroke an easy one,
but this consideration for subsequent play is still no excuse for
allowing concern for the second ball contact to diminish the
importance of that so vital first contact.

During a game, if you find that you have a little series of two
or three cannons to be played consecutively, it will probably be
because you are in a difficult position and have got into a little
bit of trouble. The thing to remember is to try to keep the two
object balls in front of you always. If you play one of these
cannons and finish between the balls, you either find that you
have to use a cushion, or involve side or screw, and immediately
the situation becomes more complicated. Of course, side and
screw have a great fascination and they might add a great
deal of pleasure to your playing, but one must also appreciate
that when you are playing at your best you will probably find
that these controls seem to be unnecessary. You are dropping
on everything nicely and the shots coming up are exactly as
you visualised them, and the use of side or screw just seems
to be superfluous. In fact, all the shots you are playing are
natural angle shots, not calling for such corrective measures.

Cushion Cannon Play
At this stage you should have developed a fair appreciation of
many shots, and the angles that the balls throw on the table.
It will become evident with a little thought, that in cushion
cannon play involving anything from one to four or five
cushions, pockets get in the way of natural angle shots. To allow
for this there has to be compensation with side, whether it be
running side or check side, to obtain the cannon. Because of the
slight variation in the throw of cushions on different tables, I
find it is quite impossible to lay down hard and fast rules as
to where a ball will strike a cushion after having been in contact
with a half-ball shot on the table. Therefore, I would like to offer
you the method of practice that I have used to improve and

99

further my ability to score cannons involving two or more cushions. I think it is a simple, practical, and interesting method, and will help you fall into gear a little quicker on tables to which you may not be accustomed.

Start by placing the red ball on the billiard spot and the cue ball on the centre spot of the 'D'. Then strike a half ball, bringing your cue ball off the top cushion, then side cushion, down to the bottom cushion and note where your cue ball strikes the bottom cushion. Having done this, place the opponent's ball on that spot. Then repeat the shot until you obtain the cannon, varying your contact on the object ball if you miss it. In this way you will gradually begin to appreciate the varying angles that the cue ball will rebound at, and where it will eventually finish.

Using this interesting method you will find that you will begin

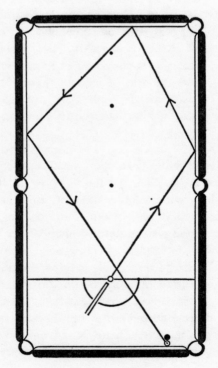

FIG 28.

to apply many little variations that appeal to you and so you will begin to formulate your own ideas of playing, and also perhaps learn something more about your own natural ability and your preferences for various parts of the table. This, I think, is a very important factor, since billards and snooker should be played according to a player's character. Either game would only have half its appeal if we all played according to the book and all looked the same when we played.

Baulk Play

Another interesting way of improving your knowledge of angles is by imagining that you are confronted with a series of double baulks by your opponent. First, place the two object balls in the baulk, fairly close together to give yourself a reasonable chance of scoring. Then play off three, four or maybe five cushions, starting from a particular spot on the baulk line, and just trying to score a cannon. This can be very absorbing and interesting. In some instances you will also find it is necessary to apply side to your ball to get around the various angles, according to where you place the two object balls.

Figures 28 and 29 show good examples of such positions for you to practise; naturally you can play variations on them. It is when you find your practice interesting and your concentration good, that time passes by quickly, and the mind is most impressed with what you are doing and stores away all the knowledge gained by such play for future occasions.

Cannon Play and Snooker

Although in the foregoing examples we have been discussing cannons pure and simple, this style of practice, interesting as it is, is still of value to the snooker player, since we are impressing on ourselves such vital matters as cushion rebound angles and the run of the ball after object-ball contact. Naturally such matters are relevant to snooker too; it could well be a snooker shot in that the object ball has been potted and the cue ball, instead of going for a cannon, is on its journey to a particular

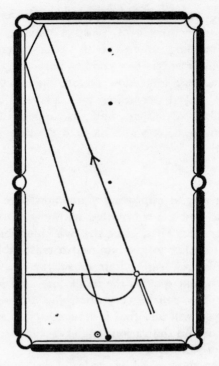

FIG 29.

part of the table to gain position for another pot. So you see that these principles can be applied to both games.

Generally speaking, cannon play in snooker demands a higher rate of accuracy, because it is essential that the pot must come off. If you do not get the pot, of course, you do not continue. Therefore, the main concentration is applied to potting the the ball, and you also endeavour to make a cannon if you possibly can. I would say before players begin to think about cannon play at snooker they should be very proficient potters, being content with the occasional cannon which is purely a natural shot and is sure to happen if they get the pot.

CHAPTER FOURTEEN

Top of the Table Technique

Perhaps it would be best to open a discussion on top of the table play by giving a gentle warning to relative beginners. Give it a trial if you like, but be prepared to pay the price if you miss, as you surely will on several occasions. You will then find that you have probably given your opponent a gift of a leave and much to your regret he is likely to make many points far too easily for your liking. If you must go to the top during a game, at the slightest sign of any trouble, and I really mean the slightest sign, come away and revert to your open game and endeavour to keep it that way.

However, now that the new billiard rule of five consecutive pots from the spot seems to have been accepted, I see no reason why the good snooker player, the type of chap who has probably always liked the odd games of billiards but has never seemed to have mastered it, should not try playing top of the table to see if he can find a new outlet for his skills. Speaking personally, I feel that billiards has been spoilt in many respects by this five-pots rule, but that again is another story.

Of course the moves at the top of the table are unlimited. They will vary according to your ability and your skill in manipulating the cue ball. The greater your command of control around the spot, so the moves become more apparent, and you will, in fact, develop moves of your own which may improve your game tremendously. However, controlling three balls around the billiard spot is undoubtedly a very difficult and delicate task. One great asset, a vital one of course, is to be a very good potter of the red ball, using where necessary screw, stun, side, stun run-through, and any other little variations that are required. A player not prepared to tackle these shots when confronted with them might just as well forget top of the table play in the true sense of the word.

Rather than delve into all the various little systems of play and variations of shot, I would like to offer a method that I have practised over the years, which I have found to be a great help, and which to some extent will eliminate a lot of complicated mental work, when you are playing. I find if you have a mental picture as to a pattern of play you can endeavour to work to this all the time, and this does help concentration. It gives you a very definite purpose, preventing you getting into constant trouble and scratching around trying to keep going.

I think that where most players seem to fall down at the top of the table is trying to maintain control of the second object ball, the opponent's ball, in a position behind the red ball for long periods. Just to explain this, let us say you are playing a sequence of pot red cannon strokes at the top, and gradually, however well you are playing, the white starts to get away from you.

This is the moment when you have to decide whether to stay at the top or go away. If the white object ball is in a really bad position, then of course you probably will have to go away. But let us say that in this case we have decided to try and rescue the white ball, and get it back behind the spot. This is the move I have employed mainly to do this.

Firstly I have an imaginary line drawn across the table $12\frac{3}{4}$ inches from the top cushion, in line with the billiard spot. During a sequence of pot red cannon play, at the first sign of the object white getting too far away from the spot, I play my next cannon in such a way that the object white is knocked up to that line on one side of the spot, either directly, or off the top cushion. You will now find when playing your next shot, a pot red, that the positioning of your cue ball for the cannon that returns the object white back to the vicinity of the spot does not have to be so precise, because of the greater variance of angle permitted by getting the object white up to that line. This method, when practised, can be used as a sequence method, which means that a little more freedom comes into your play, allowing you to stay at the top longer.

Figure 30, A-F, shows the sequence of rescuing the object white, and G-H show one of the many moves to get the object white on to that line.

Now the important thing, when you have potted the red to get your cannon position is the margin of error that your white ball has, which is so much greater than if the second object white should not be anywhere near that line. If you try setting the position up you will see that your white ball can go to quite a variation of positions and still have the same little miniature drop cannon on. You may have to use a touch of side at times, but you will find that it will give you such a greater margin for error that it takes the anxiety out of the stroke and allows you to play a little more freely. It is such little points as this which allow your game to continue at a pleasant tempo, avoiding bringing strain into the play which is, of course, what eventually lets you down.

There are many subtle moves at the top to enable you to get your object white position. If you experiment you will see what I mean. For example, you might need a little more pace on your cue ball to nudge the white up to that line, perhaps without putting power in the stroke. Very often just a little touch of running side, making the necessary allowances, will give that slight nip off the cushion and add the extra little bit of pace to the second object white to achieve this. The important thing to remember is that if you study and understand the principles of the move, you will play much more purposefully. Once you begin to have a degree of mastery of this move other moves will present themselves, and your own individual skill and ability will, of course, dictate the range of your play. You will soon begin to appreciate the importance of the delicate touch and the art of judging strength in your play, and at the top of the table you will find this invaluable.

I can recall one evening when I had two quite good billiard

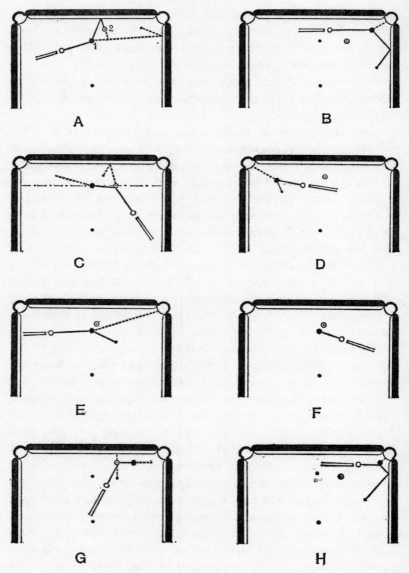

FIG 30.

players visit me for a session to improve their game at the top of the table. We had quite a successful evening. Having discussed the various points we had been through, I covered the table and we were ready to depart when the subject of strength and touch in relation to playing top of the table was raised. I said I would quickly demonstrate a point which we had spoken about and I folded the cloth back on the table 2 feet from the top cushion. I placed the red ball on the spot with the white just behind it in the position we had talked about, with the white – the cue ball – straight in line for a pot red into the corner pocket. From that position I made a 200 break without touching the folded cloth at all during the break. If you put a cloth (or a rest, or cue) across the table 2 feet from the top cushion you can test yourself in this fashion, to find out just what you are capable of.

I see no reason why, under the new rule, snooker players should not be able to turn to billiards, in fact become quite a force in the game. I am quite sure that if players would only realise this, not only would billiards be popularised but also that it would help both games, so much so that we could have quite a revival.

I have rather digressed here in my attempt to illustrate the importance of touch, but if you want to practise your touch at the top, set up the position we have been talking about, red on the spot, the white just $1\frac{1}{2}$ inches or so behind the red slightly to one side, with the cue ball in the potting position, and try to make a 50 break at the top of the table without making the second object white touch the top cushion. By trying this you will get appreciation of just how delicately one has to play, and I emphasise this, because I have tried with so many players, and some of them fairly good, to get home the point of gently dropping on to the white in a fashion that hardly moves it. This one stroke alone is so important to the game at the top of the table that it goes unnoticed. Invariably the chap playing the nice little cannon gently off the red on to the white to leave himself another pot always seems to push the white too far. Instead of just glancing across the white ball and clipping the edge of it with the edge of his white he drops full on to the second white, and knocks it too far, maybe by $1\frac{1}{2}$ inches to 2 inches. When you think that by glancing across the white ball it may only move a fraction of an inch you can see that by moving it 2 inches you have wasted maybe 10 cannons. Ten cannons means a series of ten five shots, which is fifty points.

I had this illustrated to me by one of the great players of the old days, Tom Newman, when I was just a young lad. He explained this point to me and I have been impressed by it during my playing career. I have seen it neglected by so many very good players, that I feel it is worth mentioning. Of course, the very good potter might want to pot a straight red and screw back gently, maybe six or ten inches, two or three times before playing his cannon. If he is prepared to take the risk I see no end to the scores he may be able to run up. I am quite sure within the next few years someone is going to come along who will develop this side of the game and run up some mammoth scores. Here again, we see a close relationship between the two games. This type of play should be familiar to the snooker player. Instead of potting the black he is potting a red, with all the variations and subtleties of side, stun, screw and so on. I can recollect how, in 1964, in Pukekohe, New Zealand, in the World Championship, Manny Francisco of South Africa suddenly found his touch. Being a very fine snooker player (I should also add that he is a very fine billiard player) he got to the top of the table and created the World record of 518. This was achieved mainly by potting the red, and it created quite a stir at the time, but it was a very attractive break to watch, the only difference between now and then was that at that time the ruling was 15 pots which, of course, gave even more latitude. But I still think that the present rule of five pots is quite enough to build a long break in a similar style.

CHAPTER FIFTEEN

Match Play

Every season thousands of matches are played, involving the club man who enjoys his game as a relaxation, to the local area champion, who puts more time into the game. The fact remains that when they get into the arena, things happen to both players which have an effect on their play. In the late rounds and finals the tensions can be so strong that it is the fellow with the strongest will and determination who gets through. So the question arises : does the best player always win? This is a poser without a reply; there will always be inevitable discussion on who can beat whom. This is a healthy state of affairs which helps to create such enthusiastic competition.

I have found in my experience that there are generally two types of player. One is the chap who really has to win (though I do not mean the pot hunter). He really enjoys a fight, and will soon shake off his disappointment should he lose. The other type is the more sensitive player who has the extra nice touches, which he displays in the club on a normal evening, but finds beyond his powers on the big night. Should he lose, he then suffers the agonies of being told 'Don't worry, we know you are the best player; you just didn't win'. To the budding champion, I say : learn the lesson early and recognise that losing well is not as satisfying as winning a hard fought game. Skills have to be combined with sound judgment. You have to keep control of your emotions, when it looks as if your opponent is getting all the luck. Many say you cannot alter your make up. I do not agree. Having been through the mill, I would like to justify my reasoning on this, hoping it will help someone on the way.

Like everybody else, I suffered all the various pangs of defeat and disappointments. Then I thought 'Why is it I go to work everyday and do my job consistently, in competition with everybody else, yet I don't suffer in this way, though the result could be more disastrous than that following a game of billiards or snooker?' There, to me, lay the answer. During the day I was doing my job professionally to the best of my ability. I did not worry about the other chap; I did what had to be done, at the time. When I transferred this approach to my playing, I found my concentration became stronger, I was not easily put off, and most important, it did not matter whether I was playing against a good or bad player. I just got on with the game.

Do not be embarrassed if you feel nervous and show it on the big night. Everybody does, some hide it better than others. Fight it, and you will get strength from it. Try hard right from the start. At the start of your match find a spot in the room, and when you have had your shot, return there and watch your opponent. Do not speak to others around you. They cannot help, and probably only hinder and spoil your concentration. Do the talking after the game is over.

If there was only one thing I could tell a player as he starts his game, feeling tense and apprehensive, I would say: while waiting for your turn, concentrate on your breathing. Make it deep and slow. Most top players I have met do not eat heavily before a game, which I think is right. I have always found reactions and timing are better on a fairly empty stomach. Timing, the all important factor, is co-ordination of mind and muscle. Anyway, after a good battle, what better than good food? That's the best time for it!

CHAPTER SIXTEEN

Care of Tables and Equipment

Looking After Billiard Tables

Tables are expensive items to buy and keep in good order, yet too often one sees them being spoiled sooner than need be by well-meaning club staff or officials. Firstly, when brushing a cloth, brush straight from baulk end to spot end. If the cloth is very dirty, brush with care, otherwise you will merely raise the dust which will have settled again by the time you are ready to use the iron. If the brush is used often enough, according to the amount of play on the table, this situation will not arise and the nap will retain its fresh look for much longer. Be sure the iron is hot enough, as a medium hot iron is a waste of time and does no good at all. Get the iron really hot and if in any doubt that it may be too hot, press it on a piece of paper to see that it does not scorch. Start at different sides of the table on alternate ironings. By doing this the initial heat is not always applied to the same part of the cloth, start over the spots as a variation. If the table has to be re-marked with white marking, use tailor's chalk and not the hard white pencils available, as they tend to cut into the cloth eventually, leaving grooves or holes at the markings. Always iron after you have marked out the table. Use the thin end of the brush to clean under the cushions, but do not brush the dust into the pockets. Place a duster in the pocket opening and brush into it, then remove duster and flick away any surplus. This will help to delay the inevitable wear lines into the pocket openings. With a table that is heavily used it will not hurt to brush the reverse way once in a while, thus raising the nap and removing heavy chalk marks, but you must brush again the normal way and block the table before ironing. If you have no blocking pad, wrap a piece of old billiard cloth around the brush two or three times and rub the length of the table from baulk end to spot end, until the whole surface has been treated. Care should be taken not to let the iron come into contact with the face of the cushions.

The lighting should be bright and even, not fading into shadow at the corner pockets, as this can be very distracting when judging angles. Three 150-Watt bulbs are the general requirements for lighting.

Moisture plays havoc with conditions in a billiard room, getting into the cloth and slowing down the run of the balls, and very often taking the life out of their action. You will find a dry, warm room brings the table to life, resulting in free running and lively balls, and resilient rubbers.

Selecting a Billiard Cue

Choice of cue can be a problem for the beginner because, naturally, he will not be aware of the requirements. My advice, based on what is generally accepted by good players, is to choose an ash cue, weighing from 16-18 oz., about 4 feet 7 inches to 4 feet 9 inches in length; a nice, straight piece of timber with from a 10 to 11 mm. tip with the ferrule fitted.

The wood must be well matured and the cue should not be too whippy at the tip. This you can tell by holding the butt in the right hand and giving a sharp knock on the cue with the left hand just above the hold. The top end of the cue should have a little whip, but be fairly rigid. You will find that a cue that has a lot of whip tends to push the ball off the line – which, of course, is most undesirable.

Most players will start looking for a cue that suits them when they feel they have got over the beginner's stage, and are beginning to get a lot of enjoyment from playing and are finding they can do things which they thought at first were beyond them.

They begin to think that a nice cue, which suits them, will give them added confidence.

It does not necessarily mean a new one. You may well find that you are playing with a cue you have picked out of a rack or borrowed, which is just what you need. If you can possibly acquire it (by honourable means, of course!) all well and good.

However, good quality cues are hard to find, so remember that the use and the care that you give your cue is all important. Too often you will find that when players are waiting their turn they are leaning on their cue, holding it at the tip end, causing it to bend.

Other players commit the error of putting their cue against the wall with the butt some 18-24 inches from the base of the wall, leaving it there for long periods. It is almost a certainty that a cue left like this overnight will develop a slight bend which, in most cases, cannot be removed. More cues are ruined this way than any other. I can assure you that all top players treat their cue with loving care. Take away the cue of a first-class player and you are taking away much of his ability – it is part of him.

Another point worth mentioning; you may have noticed players rubbing their cue to get it smooth with a very fine piece of sandpaper. Never do this. It is surprising how, after a period of such treatment, you can wear the cue down and it becomes whippy where it goes through your bridge hand with such constant rubbing. What you should do – only occasionally – is get a damp rag and give the cue a good hard rub. This will remove any stickiness. Then give it a good rub with a dry duster which will bring up enough natural shine from the wood to make it smooth.

Types of Cue Tip

The type of tip most suitable depends so much on individual preference. Tips can vary so much in texture and hardness that it can be a real problem to find one that suits you. You can select what seems to be a very good tip, but once you put it on your cue you find that it flatters only to deceive.

I have spent days trying to find a satisfactory replacement, my personal preference being one not too hard but good and firm, one which grips the ball when you strike it. I find that a hard tip gives the feel of allowing the ball to escape from the cue tip before you have been able to apply the effects that you want. On the other hand, a too soft tip seems to smother your intentions, though a soft tip, if you are prepared to persevere, can, over a period of time, develop into just what you require – if you can afford such time.

Still, it pays to be fastidious in your selection. I really believe tip selection can have a strong bearing on your form. Never be in a hurry to condemn a new tip, just give it time to settle down. Some can take a couple of weeks or more, so the wise player never lets himself get into the position where he is completely without a tip. I always try to keep one or two well tried ones as standbyes. This is most important, as nothing will shatter your confidence more than a tip that keeps letting you down in a vital game. When you have a suitable one look after it and occasionally rasp it very lightly with a file – but never use sandpaper. Sandpaper has a glassy content which can be harmful.

The Ball

The new Super Crystalate ball will doubtless cause some initial discussion, as happened in the early 1900s when the composition (Crystalate) ball replaced ivory, and proved far more consistent in play. The Super Crystalate has a brighter, more highly polished, harder surface – and more spring to its action. It is also approximately $\frac{1}{4}$ oz. lighter, which may cause problems with screw and forcing shots until players get used to it. When they do, I believe performances will improve – among top players, and generally, too. The 'Kick' when contact between balls is intercepted by a foreign body (it can halt the flow of play and bring a break to an end) may well be exaggerated, particularly in damp/humid conditions, so the balls must be cleaned regularly, and tables kept as free as possible from heavy chalk marks.

CHAPTER SEVENTEEN

The Billiards-Snooker Partnership

Billiards is one of the oldest of English games. It was first played several centuries ago, but it was not until the end of the nineteenth century that it began to develop towards its present form. With gradual improvement in the quality of cushions, cloth and tables in general, the game has reached its present state of high development. The golden era was from 1925 to 1937. In those days, professional tournaments, exhibitions, and matches at places like Thurstons or Burroughes Hall usually consisted of a billiards match, probably ending with a frame of snooker just to show how the game was played. Now, of course, the position is completely reversed.

The point I want to make here is that in the days when billiards was the primary game, players learnt all the various strokes and they developed the cue action through playing billiards. Then when they turned over to snooker they had all the knowledge of angle play, the cue power and all the other expertise which is required. In learning to play snooker they just had to develop accuracy of potting. Now, of course, this is difficult enough in itself but since they already had all the other basic knowledge, it did not prove half as difficult as having to learn snooker from scratch.

Today the position is rather different. In learning to play snooker first, players start, in effect, at the wrong end of the ladder. They have to try to master the hardest stroke of all, the pot, right at the outset, since potting is really the basis of all snooker.

I feel it would be much better to learn to play billiards first, since this game calls for greater variations in types of shot and playing approach. Indeed, I feel very strongly that the two games should be incorporated in any good coaching course.

As we have progressed through this book, we have first considered how to master various billiard shots, as pure shots of the game which help us to develop cue action and power, giving us at the same time, knowledge of particular shots which will lead to scoring, when actually playing a game. While learning how to concentrate on and think about strokes, we have gradually built up our techniques until we can tackle potting with confidence. As part of the process of learning how to use a cue properly, you will have tried a wide range of strokes – going in-off, scoring cannons in various ways, controlling the cue ball with side, screw and stun, making long and short pots, etc. I feel that before a player definitely selects his game, billiards or snooker, he ought to have developed the capacity to play this wide range of shots. I think this is the true way to get pleasure from a billiard table. Today it does strike me that whenever players go to a table it begins and ends with snooker. They are missing a lot of enjoyment, particularly if there is neither technique nor method in what they are doing.

On those frequent occasions when I have met good sportsmen at other games, men who seem to have all the ball sense and the timing that is called for, I have been surprised to note that when they play billiards or snooker for some relaxation they seem to have very little idea of what is required. In fact, they give the impression that it is just a question of knocking the balls around. I have always found it difficult to accept this attitude when playing any game on a billiard table. Either game is very hard to play. I would say probably among the hardest of games in the world. I cannot think of any other sport that is played to such fine limits under such controlled conditions. Consider that any match, whether it be a club match, county or world championship, demands silence, extreme care and caution; tension is long-lasting and there is just no physical release at all for the player until the end of the game.

At least when the gun is fired in athletics the competitor can release all his tensions and run like fury, and this moment of release applies to so many sports.

It is a recognised thing that a billiard player of average ability can always turn his hand to playing quite a good game of snooker, whereas a fair snooker player rarely can turn his hand to playing a good game of billiards. The billiard player will very often be in a strong position, since he can use his knowledge of angles in playing a safe game. His command of the cue ball, generally, will be better than the snooker player. Yet when it comes to the final test, the potting, we find that the snooker player so often wins the game because of his ability to recognise the pots and get them in from angles which probably are quite foreign to the billiard player. I am not trying to belittle or minimise the skill of the snooker player. I am merely trying to point out that, if the snooker player had some billiard play in his background, his snooker would probably be even better than it is. What is more, I feel that a better understanding of billiards in general would raise the overall standard of snooker amongst players everywhere. I have yet to meet the top-grade snooker player who has not been able to play a useful game of billards.

Now what I have been saying may all sound very serious and a lot of people might say, 'Good heavens, it's only a game anyway, why all this fuss about a game we just want to enjoy?' This is true about any sport, but the real enthusiast wants to go further into it, to pick up as many facts about it as he can, and to approach as near as he can to the ultimate. One has only to travel around several of the thousands of clubs in England to see the tremendous competitive spirit amongst players, predominantly at snooker. In county leagues and club championships the enthusiasm and competitive spirit is tremendous, and it is very evident that there is a craving for more knowledge.

To be able to play either game with a reasonable degree of efficiency can be one of the most satisfying and delightful of pastimes. I, personally, have found that whatever stresses and strains I may have been under at any particular time, playing a game of billiards has enabled me to leave them behind, and I know I speak for many when I say this.

Travel around the world, and I guarantee whatever town or city in which you may decide to linger, if you listen hard enough, the click of billiard balls will reach your ears. I can recall playing in Georgetown, Guyana, as guest of the Guyana Association, in their excellent club, also playing an exhibition in D'Aguiar's match room. The heat and humidity was such that good play was nigh impossible. Unlike match halls at home, the noise and exuberance of hundreds of spectators just has to be accepted, so jolly and charming are their ways. Not only do they cheer a good screw shot, some insist on interrupting proceedings to shake your hand.

Can you imagine my surprise when I was taken 70 miles up the Demerara River, to an ore-mining area, to play for the resident miners, on tables that would make your blood curdle. While names escape me, memories live forever. I shall never forget one table that had such a badly worn cloth, it had completely broken away around the spots, and to mark them, they merely made a cross chalk mark on the slate. One cushion, being void of cloth, was bound with green wool of some sort. However, so grand were the people, we all had a splendid time, and I am sure my 31 break at billiards is one of the best I have ever made. Great credit is due to Kenneth de Abreu, President of the Guyana Association, and his Council, who put on a special table, which was first class, for a big final night, before my departure.

During my stay, I held several coaching classes, for hundreds of young folk.

I recall in 1945, during the last war, sitting in the Y.M.C.A., Calcutta, watching two locals playing a very good game of billiards, one making a century break. When they finished, I asked if I might have a knock, and showing myself to be a fair player, a good time was had by all. Little did I realise I would visit there again, under much different circumstances, in 1965. I often wonder who the two players were, both extremely good.

One has only to visit Bombay and play in the clubs, to

appreciate the strength of Indian players. Wilson Jones, with whom I had the pleasure of staying, set India alight in the international field, with his great flair and dashing style, to win the World Title on two occasions, and I am sure that the present crop of young players will be following suit before long. In India, I found conditions, generally, extremely good. There are so many enthusiasts of high standard, and of course, that great stalwart for the green cloth, Mr Vissanji, of Wallace Flour Mills, is a gem to have as a leader.

I have found the Asian countries full of potential talent, but somehow only occasionally do they take the World title. I believe this is due to their desire to play the attractive game, as opposed to the match-winning, bread-and-butter game, for which I admire them.

I sat and watched Rachid Karim, the Pakistan Champion, one evening in Karachi put on a dazzling display of billiards, all around the top of the table, a joy to watch. I can well understand budding players wanting to emulate his skills, not realising that a certain gift is also needed. He and his brother Hamid, a snooker champion of equal merit, made a formidable team as organisers for the Pakistan Association. It is such people who do so much to rouse enthusiasm, in a town or country.

Take, for instance, that stalwart of the game, Frank Holz of New Zealand, who is never happy unless he is coaching youngsters or organising a tournament in some part of the world, raising funds for worthy causes. On my arrival at Auckland Airport for the World Championship in 1964, Frank met me and saw me settled in my hotel. I did not get to bed till 2 a.m., only to find Frank hammering on my door at 7 a.m., telling me I had to address the local school children after their morning prayers, at 9 a.m., with some of the other contestants. Such is the drive of this man.

One incident that I still find amusing happened in Darwin, Australia. Having had a pleasant stay with Bob O'Neil, the Australian Billiards Association President, I left for Hong Kong via Darwin, and was looking round the place when, sure enough, the click of balls came to my ears, and I entered a small clubhouse, where three burly chaps, shirtless and in bare feet, were playing snooker. I stood and watched for a while, interested in the small lizards darting in and out of cracks, catching flies. I couldn't help laughing to myself, but unfortunately the players thought I was laughing at them. I was immediately challenged to put my money down or else. Needless to say, I did not put my money down. I made my apologies and left, and was thankful to get out in one piece, to continue on a pleasant journey, playing and meeting different people, and finding how much alike we all are, when the barriers are down.

It is with such thoughts in mind that I have put this book together. All the points I have talked about are quite basic ones. I have not gone into the deeper side and technicalities of the game. The build up of practice strokes is the surest way to bring a measure of success and pleasure to the less talented.

I hope, too, that I have helped to satisfy the player, who, though he knows he will never make it as a top flighter himself, gets a great deal of pleasure out of discussing the complicated reactions of side, screw, and nap, top of the table play at billiards, or an 'impossible' pot at snooker. He derives his pleasure from being able to discuss and understand what happens when he is watching top-flight players. I have always found this type of person to be among the most genuine supporters of the green cloth, in fact, the backbone of the game. Throughout the world I have met such true enthusiasts, and their love of the game is unsurpassed in any other sport.